## Lernkrimi Englisch

# Murder at Teatime

### Alison Romer
### Oliver Astley

**circon**

# Vokabeltraining
## zum Buch!

Lerne die Vokabeln zu diesem Buch: Mit phase6, Deutschlands führenden Vokabeltrainer.

Mit phase6 übst du deine Vokabeln über Computer, Tablet und Smartphone mit Android oder iOS.

**Der Circon Verlag schenkt dir die erste Vokabelsammlung zu seinen Büchern. Nur erhältlich über diesen Link (QR-Code).**

www.phase6.de/s/a2855

 **Der beste Sprachtrainer für die Schule.**

© Circon Verlag GmbH
Baierbrunner Str. 27, 81379 München
Ausgabe 2023
4. Auflage

Redaktion: Sarah Portner
Fachkorrektur: Nathalie Russell, Vanessa Magson-Mann
Produktion: Ute Hausleiter
Titelillustration: Karl Knospe
Lernkrimi-Logo: Carsten Abelbeck
Gestaltung: EKH Werbeagentur GbR, textum GmbH
Umschlaggestaltung: red.sign GbR, Stuttgart

ISBN 978-3-8174-1856-5
381741856/4

Besuchen Sie uns auf Instagram und Facebook: circonverlag
www.circonverlag.de

 **Vorwort**

Liebe Leserin, lieber Leser,

sicher zum Lernerfolg – mit Spaß und Spannung! Die Compact Lernkrimis mit ihrer Kombination aus Lektüre und didaktischem Übungsanteil eignen sich hervorragend, um breite Sprachkompetenzen in der Fremdsprache zu erwerben. Der Lernende wird dabei durch die spannende Handlung, das angemessene Sprachniveau und den stetig ansteigenden Schwierigkeitsgrad der Übungen gefördert und motiviert.

Entwickelt nach neuesten Erkenntnissen der Fremdsprachendidaktik, sind Compact Lernkrimis das ideale Medium für einen Lernerfolg im Selbststudium. Durch die kleinen Texteinheiten und den hohen Übungsanteil sind sie aber auch als Unterrichtslektüre bestens geeignet.

**So lernen Sie mit Compact Lernkrimis:**

- **Mit Begeisterung lernen:** Die packende Krimihandlung motiviert Sie beim Lesen des englischen Originaltextes.
- **Wissen intensivieren und erweitern:** Durch die Kombination aus didaktisch aufbereiteter Lektüre und textbezogenen Übungen testen und trainieren Sie Ihre Sprachkenntnisse effektiv. Vokabelangaben auf jeder Seite unterstützen Sie beim Lesen.
- **Systematisch lernen:** Knüpfen Sie an Ihr individuelles Sprachniveau an und setzen Sie eigene Lernziele.
- **Unabhängig sein:** Lernen Sie individuell – wo und wann immer Sie wollen.

Viel Spaß beim **spannenden Erlernen der englischen Sprache** wünscht Ihnen

Prof. Dr. Christiane Neveling
Didaktik der romanischen Sprachen, Universität Leipzig

# Inhalt

Murder at Teatime ............................................................ 5

A Model Murder ............................................................. 43

A Family Affair ............................................................. 85

Final Test ................................................................. 128

Answers ................................................................. 133

Glossary ................................................................. 139

List of Exercises ........................................................... 154

# Murder
# at Teatime

**Alison Romer**

# A Village Death

Ida McBride sits at the table with a nice cup of tea in her hands. While she drinks her tea, she looks at the lovely flowers on the table. There are some pink roses and some yellow lilies. They are a **gift** from Mavis Hammond. Mavis grows lots of flowers in her garden. She also bakes cakes and makes jam. She's a very busy woman, and very active for a 70-year-old. Normally, Ida is busy, too. Now she can't go to church or visit her friends. Sometimes she feels too sick to eat. The doctor says Ida should **rest**. He thinks it's normal for a 72-year-old woman to feel a bit tired and sick. But this is the fourth week she feels too sick to go out, and she's very unhappy about it.

Suddenly, Ida hears a siren. She slowly stands up and goes to the window. She moves the **lace curtains** and looks outside. An **ambulance** comes up the street and stops in front of her neighbours' house. Two **paramedics** jump out. They **rush** into the house. Ida's neighbours are Mark and Lydia King. They are both around forty years old and normally very quiet. Ida is worried and stands looking out of the window until she sees the paramedics come out. They are carrying a **stretcher** with Mark King

| | |
|---|---|
| gift | Geschenk |
| to rest | (sich) (aus)ruhen |
| lace curtain | Spitzengardine |
| ambulance | Krankenwagen |
| paramedic | Rettungssanitäter |
| to rush | eilen, rasen |
| stretcher | Tragbahre |

on it. His wife, Lydia, runs out of the house. The paramedics put Mark in the back of the ambulance and Lydia gets into the ambulance with them. Then the sirens start again and the ambulance drives away.

| | |
|---|---|
| sergeant | Polizeimeisterin |
| file | Akte; Datei |
| antiques dealer | Antiquitäten-händler |
| heart attack | Herzinfarkt |
| potassium | Kalium |
| kidney | Niere |

Four days later, Detective Inspector Weyland Green is in his office at the Cambridge Police Station. He is sitting at his desk and looking at an autopsy report. After fifteen minutes, he stands up and goes to make some fresh coffee. While he is waiting for the coffee to be ready, he hears a knock at the door.

"Come in," he says.

Detective Sergeant Miranda Coleman opens the door.

"Hello," she says. "You wanted to see me, Inspector?"

"Yes," DI Green says and gives her a file. "An antiques dealer named Mark King has died in the village of Little Barnswold. He was a bit young, only forty-six, but it looked like a heart attack at first. The pathologist sent me a report after the autopsy."

"It wasn't a heart attack, was it?" asks Miranda.

"No," says the inspector. [i] "The autopsy shows that there was too much potassium in his kidneys."

"Did he have a history of kidney problems?"

"Yes, and he took medication," DI Green answers. "But it wasn't

> Namen und Titel werden im Englischen großgeschrieben. Dies gilt, wenn eine Person direkt angesprochen wird oder der Titel in Verbindung mit dem Namen verwendet wird.
> *"You wanted to see me, Inspector?"* oder *"Inspector Weyland Green is in his office."*
> Erscheint der Titel jedoch ohne direkte Ansprache im fortlaufenden Text, wird er kleingeschrieben.
> *"No," says the inspector.*

the medicine that killed him. The pathologist **suspects** it was **poison**."

DI Green **pours** two cups of coffee. He pours milk into one of the cups and gives it to Miranda.

"I'd like you to help me on this **case**, Sergeant."

"Thanks. I'd be happy to," Miranda says.

"Our **forensic scientists** are trying to identify the poison," Inspector Green says.

He drinks some of his coffee.

"I think we should go to Little

| | |
|---|---|
| **to suspect** | verdächtigen, einen Verdacht haben |
| **poison** | Gift |
| **to pour** | einschenken, schütten |
| **case** | Fall; Tasche, Hülle |
| **forensic scientist** | Gerichtsmediziner |
| **crime scene** | Tatort |
| **to enjoy sth.** | etw. genießen, Freude haben an etw. |
| **vicarage** | Pfarrhaus |
| **grocery shop** | Lebensmittelgeschäft |
| **chemist** | Apotheke |

Barnswold this afternoon and talk to Mark King's wife. Ask the **crime scene** team to come, too, Sergeant Coleman. Then get the car. I'll finish my coffee."

"No problem, sir. I'll call them right away. There is nothing like a nice trip to the country," Miranda smiles.


The village of Little Barnswold is twenty-five kilometres from Cambridge. The countryside is beautiful and the inspector **enjoys** the drive. It is so different from the city, which has a lot of traffic and a lot of tourists. The village is very small. It has a church and a **vicarage**, and there are about thirty-five houses in total. There is one pub called The Rose and Crown. On the main street there is a post office, a **grocery shop** and a **chemist**. There is also Mark King's antique shop.

Miranda uses the navigation system to find the Kings' house on Crocus Street. It's a lovely old cottage. There is a white Mercedes in the driveway and a black one parked on the street.

"Very nice," says Miranda, as she parks the police car on the street in front of the house.

| | |
|---|---|
| driveway | Einfahrt |
| rug | (kleiner) Teppich, Vorleger |
| half-day closing | halber freier Tag |

She and DI Green get out. They see the curtains in the house next door move and an old lady looking out of the window.

"The neighbour," says DI Green. "We should talk to her. Old ladies know everything that happens in a village."

"Yes, sir," says Miranda. She knocks on the door of the Kings' cottage. A thin woman with blonde hair opens it.

"Mrs King?" Miranda asks.

"Yes," says the woman. "I'm Lydia King."

She's about 45 years old and is wearing jeans and a pink T-shirt. She has lots of make-up on, but she looks very tired.

"This is Detective Inspector Green, and I'm Sergeant Coleman. We would like to talk to you about your husband."

"Yes, of course," says Mrs King. "Please come in."

The living room of the cottage is full of antique furniture. There are old paintings on the walls and a beautiful Turkish rug in front of the open fireplace. It is summer so there is no fire, but a large grey cat is lying on the rug.

"Would you like something to drink?" Mrs King asks.

"No, thanks," says DI Green.

He sits down on the leather sofa and Miranda sits next to him. Mrs King sits in a comfortable antique armchair. Miranda takes out her notebook.

"First, can you tell us about the day Mr King died?" asks DI Green. "It's important that you tell us as many details as possible."

"It was a completely normal day," Mrs King says. "Mark got up at seven o'clock and then went to his shop as usual at around eight. It was half-day closing, so he came home at half past twelve and we had lunch together."

"What did he have for lunch?" asks the inspector.

"He had egg and chips," she replies. "He didn't eat breakfast that day. He just had a coffee."

| to exclaim | (aus)rufen |
| custard tart | Vanilletörtchen |
| to lose weight | abnehmen |
| to collapse | zusammen-brechen |
| confused | verwirrt |

"Did you eat the same thing?" DI Green asks.

"No!" **exclaims** Mrs King. "I eat healthy food. I had a salad with some fresh fruit. I cooked Mark's food but I never ate it. The doctor said Mark should eat healthy food, but he didn't."

"And did he feel sick after lunch?" asks DI Green.

"Mark didn't feel well for the last two weeks. He didn't want to eat a lot. I told him to go back to the doctor."

"What else happened?"

"He went upstairs and watched TV in bed. I went to the gym. I got home at half past three. At four o'clock Mark came downstairs again and ate a **custard tart**. He had afternoon tea at four every day. He loved cakes and biscuits, even when he felt sick. He was getting really fat, but this illness made him **lose weight**."

"You told the paramedics that Mr King **collapsed** at around 4:20 p.m.," says DI Green.

"That's right," replies Mrs King. "I was so scared. He stood up from the table and then collapsed on the floor. I called the ambulance."

"You called the ambulance at 4:43," Miranda says, looking at her notebook. "What were you doing for those twenty minutes, Mrs King?"

Mrs King is **confused**. She looks at DI Green.

"I tried to wake Mark up. I shook him and called his name, but he didn't answer and he didn't move. Then I poured water on his face. I tried to give him his kidney medication."

"Did you love your husband?" asks the inspector.

Mrs King jumps out of her chair.

"Of course I did!" she shouts. "He was my husband!"

The cat wakes up and runs up the stairs.

| | |
|---|---|
| to gasp | keuchen, nach Luft schnappen |
| to accuse sb. | jmd. beschuldigen |
| to treat | behandeln |
| suspicious | verdächtig; misstrauisch |
| to poison sb. | jmd. vergiften |

"Please calm down, Mrs King," says DI Green. "We just need information right now. A crime scene team will be here soon. They'll take food from your cupboards and fridge and medication from your bathroom."

"You think I killed my husband!" Mrs King gasps. She is very shocked and her face turns as white as a sheet.

"I'm not accusing you of anything. But we are treating his death as suspicious. He was poisoned."

Mrs King sits down on the sofa again. She puts her head in her hands.

"No," she says. "I don't believe it."

---

**Exercise 1: Simple Past.** Setzen Sie die folgenden unregelmäßigen Verben ins Simple Past.

1. make _____
2. have _____
3. put _____

4. feel _____
5. eat _____
6. do _____

---

After the crime scene team arrive, DI Green and Miranda go back to the car.

"Mrs King cooked all her husband's food," says Miranda. "And there is that 20-minute **gap** between Mr King collapsing and Mrs King calling the ambulance. That doesn't look good."

"The scene team will take everything for testing," says the inspector. "They'll take the Kings' rubbish, too. It's possible that Mrs King threw away the poison before she called the ambulance."

| gap | Lücke |
| --- | --- |
| suspect | Verdächtiger |
| last will and testament | Testament |
| filing cabinet | Aktenschrank |

"Do you think she did it?" asks Miranda.

"The husband or wife is always the first **suspect**, but we need a motive. Can you find out about King's **last will and testament**?"

They drive back through the village. DI Green wants to stop at the antique shop.

"I've got the keys from the crime scene team," the inspector says. "I think we should look around."

Together, he and Miranda walk through the shop. It is full of beautiful antique furniture, paintings, mirrors and vases.

"I want you to go through King's business papers, too," DI Green tells Miranda.

They go into the office at the back of the shop. There are two big **filing cabinets** and a desk full of papers.

"I can't take all these back to the station," says Miranda. "I'll come back tomorrow morning and look at them here."

"Good idea."

They leave the shop, lock it up again and get back into the car.

"Back to Cambridge!" says Miranda, happily. "I don't like little villages. They look sweet, but you don't know what happens behind closed doors!"

"Well, I like it here," says DI Green. "No tourists and no bicycles! Just afternoon tea and a walk in the countryside afterwards."

"You have a very romantic idea about country life, Inspector," laughs Miranda.

"And you've read too many Agatha Christie books!" replies DI Green. "You think village life is all murder and little old ladies!"

"Old ladies!" Miranda exclaims. "What?"

"We forgot to talk to the neighbour!"

"Next time," says the inspector. "She's not Miss Marple, you know!"

| | |
|---|---|
| to wave | schwenken, winken |
| to brake | bremsen |
| collar | Kragen |
| reverend | Pfarrer, Pastor |
| airy | luftig |
| stained-glass window | Buntglasfenster |
| community | Gemeinde |

As they drive past the church, a man in black suddenly runs out onto the street. He is **waving** his arms wildly. Miranda **brakes** because she thinks the man is going to run in front of the car, but he doesn't. When the car stops, he comes up to Miranda's window and she rolls it down. He is wearing a black jacket and a black pullover with the white **collar** of a **reverend**.

"You're Detective Inspector Green and Sergeant Coleman, aren't you?" the man asks.

Before they have time to reply, the man speaks again. "I'm Reverend Matthew Davies. Can I speak with you for a moment?"

"Yes, of course," says the DI politely.

The three of them go into the church. It's large and **airy**, with pretty **stained-glass windows** and some children's paintings on the walls.

"Our church is the centre of the **community**," says the reverend. "Not everybody who comes here is religious, but we have a lot of family events and social clubs. We also have a café. It's the only café in Little Barnswold. We do a lovely afternoon tea."

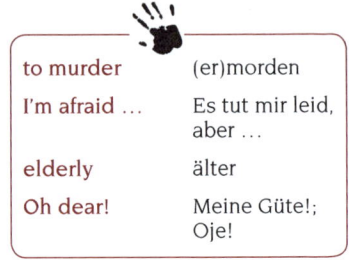

| to murder | (er)morden |
| I'm afraid … | Es tut mir leid, aber … |
| elderly | älter |
| Oh dear! | Meine Güte!; Oje! |

"That's very nice, Reverend," DI Green says. "However, we're quite busy. What did you want to speak to us about?"

"Oh," says Reverend Davies, looking nervous. "Sorry, Inspector Green. I called the Cambridge police station and they told me you would be here today. You believe Mark King was murdered, don't you?"

"We're treating his death as suspicious, yes," replies DI Green. The reverend puts his hand on the inspector's arm.

"I have some information that might be important," he says.

---

**Exercise 2: Questions.** Formulieren Sie die passenden Fragen zu folgenden Antworten. Verwenden Sie ein Fragewort und **did**!

what    how    who    when    why    where

**1.** I ate a sandwich.      *What did you eat?*

**2.** I went to the shops.      _____

**3.** I called to say hello.      _____

**4.** I met Mrs King.      _____

**5.** I got here by train.      _____

**6.** I went there this morning. _____

Suddenly the door of the church opens. An old lady comes in, carrying a big basket of flowers.

"Hello, Reverend!" she says. "The flowers are here! The others are in my car."

"Hello, Mavis," says the reverend. "I'm afraid I need to talk to these people privately. Could you wait in the café for a few minutes?"

"Of course," says Mavis. "I'll ask one of the ladies to help me with the flowers. We can bring them in through the back door."

"Thank you."

Mavis goes out again and shuts the big church door behind her.

"She's very nice," Reverend Davies says to DI Green and Miranda. "All of our elderly ladies are very nice. Mavis Hammond does the flowers for the church. She grows most of them in her garden. It's wonderful! Of course, Ida McBride is normally our flower lady, but she's sick at the moment. Mavis is usually one of our cleaning ladies. She's taken over Ida's job until Ida gets better."

"That's very interesting, Reverend Davies," says DI Green, "but you have some information. What is it?"

"I can't give you many details," the reverend replies. "I just know that Lydia… that is, Mrs King… she… oh dear."

"Can you be clear, Reverend?" asks Miranda.

"Well, I believe that she's friends with a man from the next village. Very good friends."

"You mean she has a lover?" asks Miranda.

The reverend's face goes red.

"Unfortunately, I think so," he says, sadly. "And he's not a very nice man."

15

# 2 Lies

The next day, DI Green and the sergeant arrive back in Little Barnswold and park the car outside Mark King's antique shop. Miranda goes inside to look through King's business papers while the inspector takes a walk to the church.

He opens the big door and goes inside. At the altar an elderly lady is arranging flowers into a beautiful big display of purple lilac and white roses. The inspector recognizes her.

| | |
|---|---|
| lilac | Flieder |
| to recognize | (wieder) erkennen |
| funeral | Beerdigung |
| to release | freigeben, freilassen |
| counter | Theke, Ladentheke |
| scone | brötchenartiges Teegebäck |
| to treat oneself to sth. | sich etw. gönnen |

"Hello!" the lady says.

"Hello," replies DI Green. "You're Mavis Hammond, right?"

"Yes, I am. Do you want to speak to the reverend?"

"No, I've come for a cup of coffee. Those are beautiful flowers."

"Thank you, dear," Mavis says. "I grow them in my own garden. I want to use lilac for the funeral of our Mr King, too. The village is waiting for the police to release his body. We all want to say goodbye."

"Of course," says the inspector.

> **Scones**, ein weiches Gebäck, werden in Großbritannien meist warm mit Butter und Konfitüre gegessen. Besonders zum traditionellen *afternoon tea* genießt man sie auch mit einer Art dickem Streichrahm (*clotted cream*). Angeblich das Lieblingsessen der Queen.

"You don't expect the young ones to go first," Mavis goes on. "You think old people like me will die first, but some of them just keep going and going…"

"Sorry, Mavis, can you tell me where the café is?" asks the inspector quickly. "I have an appointment."

**Exercise 3: Translation.** Lesen Sie weiter und übersetzen Sie die deutschen Begriffe!

The church café is small but very **1. hübsch** _____

_____. The walls are stone, and **2. durch**

_____ the tiny windows the inspector can see the vicarage garden. All the tables have white tablecloths with little vases of **3. Blumen** _____,

and there is a counter full of delicious-looking cakes and scones.[i] The DI thinks that, even though he is working on

a **4. Fall** _____, he can treat himself to a

scone. Or **5. vielleicht** _____ two scones. He sits down. An old lady with glasses and curly white hair comes to his table.

"What **6. kann** _____ I get you?" she says.

"I'd like a cup of coffee and a scone with **7. Marmelade**

_____ and cream," DI Green says.

"I think tea tastes better with scones," the woman says. "The classic English Cream Tea. We do the best in Cambridgeshire!"

"I'm afraid I don't drink tea," replies the inspector.

"Never?" the old lady asks.

"Absolutely never," Green says, smiling.

The inspector is starting to eat his scone when suddenly a man sits down at his table. Green looks up.

"Craig Lowry?" he says.

"You wanted to talk to me?" asks the man.

"Yes, I'm Detective Inspector Green. Thank you for meeting me here."

"I didn't have much choice,"

| | |
|---|---|
| **criminal record** | Vorstrafen-register |
| **to beat up** | zusammen-schlagen |
| **violence** | Gewalt |
| **to sip** | nippen, trinken |

says Lowry. "Either here or at the station, that's what you said."

"Would you like some coffee?"

"No, let's just get on with it. What do you want from me?"

"Well," says the inspector, taking a bite from his scone. "You've got a **criminal record**, you've spent time in prison for **beating up** a man, you've got a history of **violence**, and your ex-wife called the police on you twice."

"I know all this," says Lowry. "What are you saying?"

"Mark King is dead. You are having an affair with his wife," DI Green says. "I'm wondering if there is any connection between these two things."

He **sips** his coffee and eats a bit more of his scone.

"I don't know what you're talking about. I'm not having an affair with King's wife," Lowry says, looking angry. "I don't even know her."

"I believe you do," says Green. "I can hold you in a police cell for twenty-four hours, so it's much better if you tell me the truth now."

Craig Lowry looks worried.

"Can we have another cup of coffee over here?" Green calls to the lady behind the counter.

The two men sit in silence until the woman brings the coffee and puts it in front of Lowry. He pours in a lot of sugar and milk and then sips it quickly.

"Okay," he says. "Okay, it's true. Lydia and I are together. She planned to leave King in a few weeks to be with me. But we didn't kill him! That's the truth."

"I need you to make an official **statement** about that," Green tells him. "I'll get an officer to

| statement | Aussage, Erklärung |
| to slam the door | die Tür zuknallen |
| receipt | Quittung |
| record | Aufzeichnung, Aufnahme |
| purchase | Kauf |

talk to you and write down what you say. Then you can read it and sign it."

"I'm not making any statements!" Lowry speaks in a very low voice. "Leave me alone and leave Lydia alone!"

He pushes back his chair and stands up. Then he walks out of the café quickly, **slamming the door** behind him.

DI Green calmly eats the last bite of his scone. He is thinking about ordering another one when the door opens again. It is Sergeant Coleman, who is carrying a big file of papers. She hurries over to the inspector's table and sits down.

"There's something strange going on, sir," she says.

Together, they look at the papers from the antique shop.

"Let me explain what's wrong," says Miranda. "Look, here we have **receipts** for some furniture that King sold. Two tables and an armchair, sold on July 29th and August 2nd. The problem is that there's no **record** of **purchase** for any of these things."

"Do you mean that King never bought them but he still sold them?" asks the DI.

"Right," replies Miranda. She puts some yellow papers in front of the inspector. "Now, look here. It seems that he did buy some furniture. Here are some purchase records for furniture King bought between December and June 2008. He bought it from different people on different dates. A side table and two **candlesticks** on January 18th in the village of

| | |
|---|---|
| candlestick | Kerzenständer |
| chandelier | Kronleuchter |
| consecutive | aufeinander-folgend |

Fen Ditton. A Louis XVII chair on May 26th in Grantchester. A **chandelier**, also in Fen Ditton, on June 1st."

---

**Exercise 4: Negation.** Schreiben Sie die Verneinung für folgende Sätze auf!

1. He bought two tables.

   _He didn't buy two tables._

2. She's having an affair with him.

3. You've got a criminal record.

4. I'll listen to you.

5. The inspector eats his scone.

---

"So what's the matter with these records?" asks Green.

"The numbers on the receipts are **consecutive**, Inspector," replies Miranda. "The January 18th number is 100569, the June number is 100570. But here, look, the May 26th number is 100571. That's not normal."

"No," agrees DI Green. "It looks as if someone has made purchase receipts for each **item** of furniture, one after the other."

"Exactly," says the sergeant. "Someone has **invented** the dates. I'm worried that the names are invented, too. Probably to hide something illegal. I'm going to look up all the names and addresses in our database. And we should visit some of these people and ask them about King."

| item | Gegenstand, Artikel |
| to invent | erfinden |
| mood | Laune |
| to stretch | (sich) strecken |
| to yawn | gähnen |

"I agree. Good job, Sergeant. But now I think I should go and visit Mrs King again. Let's see if she's in a better **mood** when I ask her about Craig Lowry."

The inspector pays for his coffee and scone and says goodbye to the lady with the glasses. They walk back through the church and out to the car. Miranda drives them to the Kings' house. She decides to stay in the car to keep working on the purchase receipts.

Inspector Green walks up to the door and rings the bell. He sees someone look out of the window, but nothing happens. He waits a minute and then rings the bell again. Finally, Lydia King opens the door.

"How can I help you this time, Inspector?"

"I'd like to come in, Mrs King," DI Green replies. "We need to talk."

"Is that really necessary?"

"I'm afraid it is," says the DI.

Mrs King moves out of the way and lets the inspector go inside. She follows him. The cat is on the rug again, and it **stretches**

> Tiere sind im Englischen sächlich. Daher verwendet man für sie das Pronomen **it**. Handelt es sich allerdings um Haustiere mit Namen, benutzt man **he** und **she**.

and **yawns**. The inspector sits on the sofa and looks around at all

the beautiful antique furniture. He wonders where it came from.
"Have you found out why my husband died?"
"We're working on it," DI Green says. "And you can help by telling us about your relationship with Mr Craig Lowry."

**Exercise 5: Choose the correct alternative.** Lesen Sie weiter und unterstreichen Sie die richtige Variante!

Mrs King looks the inspector straight in the eye.

"I don't 1. have / had a relationship with Craig Lowry."

"That's not what he says."

"Well, he's 2. lieing / lying !" Mrs King exclaims.

"Oh, come on, Mrs King," says Green, standing up, "you can stop **pretending**. I've 3. talking / talked to Lowry and he's told me all about it. If you keep **denying** it, it just 4. makes / does things worse. I'll think you've got 5. somewhere / something to hide, like murdering your husband."

"But I didn't!"

"If you are **innocent**, you don't 6. need to / must worry," says the inspector. "I'm just 7. asked / asking you to come to the station. An officer 8. wants / will interview you and take a formal statement. I'm not **arresting** you - yet. But I've got to tell you that you're my **prime suspect** right now."

Now Mrs King stands up, too.

"I'll come to the station," she says. "I want to **prove** to you all that I'm innocent."

"Then come to the main Cambridge station any time today or this evening."

Later that afternoon, DI Green and Sergeant Coleman sit in the car and look at the list of names from King's purchase receipts. Miranda sets the navigation system for an address in Fen Ditton, a pretty village just outside Cambridge. It doesn't take long for the inspector and Miranda to get there. They find the right address and park the car outside.

| | |
|---|---|
| to pretend | vorgeben, vortäuschen |
| to deny | leugnen |
| innocent | unschuldig |
| to arrest | verhaften |
| prime suspect | Hauptverdächtige |
| to prove | beweisen |
| odd | seltsam, komisch |
| stately home | Herrenhaus |
| ordinary | normal, gewöhnlich |
| semi-detached (house) | Doppelhaushälfte |

"This is **odd**," says Miranda. "This is Mary Walsh's house, isn't it? The receipt says King bought a Louis XVII chair here on May 26th. But I can't believe the person who lives here has such expensive antique furniture."

"I agree," says the DI. "I was expecting a **stately home**, too."

The Walsh house is an **ordinary semi-detached** with a little garden in the front and an old car parked outside.

Together they walk up to the house and ring the little bell. An old lady answers the door.

"Hello?" she says, smiling.

She looks at Sergeant Coleman's police uniform and stops smiling.

"Is there something wrong?" the old lady asks.

"We were wondering if you sold a Louis XVII chair in May last year?" DI Green says.

"A what?"

Green and Miranda look at each other. Miranda explains about the purchase receipt and the antique chair.

"I most certainly did not sell anything," the woman says. "I bought my sofa and chairs fifteen years ago, just before my husband died. I've never sold any furniture."

After thanking the old lady for

| to head for | zusteuern auf |
| burglary | Einbruch |
| to drop sb. off | jmd. absetzen |
| to research | untersuchen, erforschen |
| overtime | Überstunden |
| channel | Kanal |

her help, the inspector and Miranda get back into the car and head for the next address on the list. It takes them just over two hours to visit six people. At every house, it is the same story.

"Nobody sold the furniture recorded in the purchase receipts," says Miranda on their way back to Cambridge. "The details are all invented but the furniture is real. King sold it for a lot of money. The only question is, where did he get it?"

DI Green asks Miranda to create a list of King's purchases and sales and then compare them with burglaries in the area. On her way back to the police station, Miranda drops Green off at his house in the city.

"I'll start researching burglaries tonight, sir," she says. "I can do with the overtime. I want a holiday in Greece this year!"

"I think I'll spend my holiday in Little Barnswold," says the inspector. "I like it there."

They arrange to meet the next day at the station and say goodbye.

Once inside, DI Green puts the TV on. He changes channels to find the news, then he goes into the kitchen and pours himself a glass of whisky. He opens the fridge and takes out a ready meal: salmon fillet with spinach and potatoes au gratin. He watches the news while he waits for his dinner to heat up in the microwave.

At about 10:30 his phone rings. He is asleep on the sofa with the TV on and an empty plate resting on his stomach. The sound of the phone wakes him up.

"It's Sergeant Coleman," says Miranda quickly. "I've got some news. I've arrested both Lydia King and Craig Lowry, and I'm holding them at the station for 24 hours. I need you to come in tomorrow and talk to them."

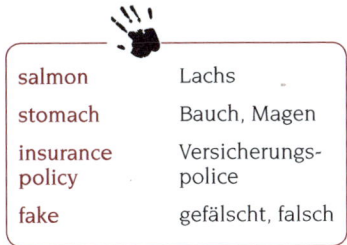

| salmon | Lachs |
| stomach | Bauch, Magen |
| insurance policy | Versicherungs- police |
| fake | gefälscht, falsch |

"Do you have a good reason to hold them?" the inspector asks.

"Oh, absolutely," replies Miranda. "Lydia will get almost two million pounds from Mark King's insurance policy, and there are two flights booked to Barbados for next week."

"Two flights? Let me guess," says DI Green, "Lydia King and Lowry."

"Right," Miranda answers.

"And the antique furniture? Any news about that?"

"Yes, I've also been looking at records and reports of antiques burglaries and we were right, sir. Most of the furniture in the fake purchase receipts was stolen during the last two years. It looks as if Mark King ran a stolen antiques business."

"Did Lydia King know?" asks Green. "I wonder. I'll ask her tomorrow. I'll be at the station at lunchtime."

# 3 Suspects

DI Weyland Green is in heaven. He's never seen anything more wonderful in his life, he thinks.

"It's all homemade!" says the old lady with the white hair.

The inspector smiles. "Mmm, delicious."

He picks up his fork and **digs into** a huge piece of chocolate cake filled with chocolate cream and **coated with** chocolate **icing**. It is the best he has ever had in his life. Next to it is a cup of coffee. He is just taking a sip when the reverend comes into the café.

"Second breakfast?" asks Reverend Davies, looking at the chocolate cake.

Inspector Green laughs.

**Exercise 6: Prepositions.** Setzen Sie die richtige Präposition ein!

down    into    from    on (2x)    to    up

1. Lowry was in prison for beating [          ] a man.
2. The furniture came [          ] France.
3. Please calm [          ].
4. You must come [          ] the station.
5. Look at the numbers [          ] the receipts.
6. He digs [          ] the cake.
7. We're working [          ] it.

"How is the **investigation** going?" the reverend asks and sits down at the table.

"I'm glad you asked," says the DI, serious again. "I have some questions about Mark King's antiques business. I can't find any record of his **employees**. Do you know if anyone worked with him? Perhaps his wife?"

"No, Lydia didn't work with Mark," says the reverend. "You know, Inspector, she isn't the kind of woman to work. I know that sounds like a criticism, but

| | |
|---|---|
| ⚡ to dig into | sich stürzen auf |
| coated with | überzogen mit |
| icing | Zuckerguss |
| investigation | Ermittlung, Untersuchung |
| employee | Angestellter |
| marriage | Ehe |
| law | Gesetz |
| taxes *pl* | Steuern |
| ⚡ taxman | Finanzamt |

she and Mark had an old-fashioned **marriage**. Lydia looked after the house and Mark made the money."

"So who did work with him?"

"As far as I know, some young men from this and the next village," Reverend Davies replies. "I can give you their names."

"Thanks, that would be great," says DI Green.

He takes another bite of chocolate cake and then takes out his notebook. Reverend Davies gives him a few names of men who live nearby.

"I'm afraid they were working 'unofficially', if you know what I mean," he continues more carefully. "I hope they won't get into too much trouble with the **law**."

"Don't worry, right now I'm more interested in murder," Green says. "I'll leave **taxes** to the **taxman**."

Suddenly the inspector's phone rings. It is Sergeant Coleman.

"I've got some news, sir. We know what poisoned King. The pathology team got the test results back."

"What is it?"

"**Digoxin**," answers Miranda. "Digoxin poisoning causes an overdose of potassium in the kidneys. An early symptom is **nausea**, and King felt sick for several weeks. The only problem is that **forensics** haven't found digoxin in any of the food or chemicals from the Kings' house."

"I'm going to go back to the house myself," says the inspector. "I want to have another look around."

"I'll come with you," says Miranda. "I'll leave Cambridge now and meet you at the Kings' house. I'll bring the keys."

**Exercise 7: Adjectives. Lesen Sie weiter und unterstreichen Sie die zwölf Adjektive im folgenden Abschnitt!**

An hour later, the DI and Sergeant Coleman open the door of the Kings' lovely cottage and go inside. Both of them pull on fresh latex **gloves**.

"Let's start in the kitchen," says the inspector.

Suddenly the grey cat appears and starts **meowing**.

"I think he's hungry," says Miranda while she **strokes** the cat's head."

The kitchen is very big with lots of expensive **appliances** and **shiny** pots. In the middle is a large antique table.

"Wouldn't you love to have a beautiful kitchen like this?" says Miranda.

"What would I do with it?" replies DI Green, opening the small cupboard under the **sink**.

"Cook wonderful meals!" says Miranda.

The inspector shakes his head. "That's what ready-meals are for," he says.

The inspector stands up. "Well, there's nothing under the sink. I think the crime scene team got it all."

He moves over to the cupboards. Inside there are lots of tins and jars. One by one he takes them out, looks at them and puts them on the floor. None of them have been opened.

Meanwhile, Miranda takes everything out of the fridge and the freezer. There is not much

| | |
|---|---|
| digoxin | Digoxin (aus Fingerhut gewonnener giftiger Wirkstoff) |
| nausea | Übelkeit |
| forensics | Spurensicherung |
| gloves *pl* | Handschuhe |
| to meow | miauen |
| to stroke | streicheln |
| appliance | Gerät |
| shiny | glänzend, leuchtend |
| sink | Spülbecken |
| tin | Dose, Büchse |
| jar | Einmachglas |
| raspberry | Himbeere |
| blackberry | Brombeere |
| evidence | Beweis(e) |

in the fridge. It is all at the forensics laboratory. There are lots of packages in the freezer, however, and the sergeant carefully looks at each one. She checks to see if they are open, but none of them are.

The inspector finds a jar of jam. It is homemade jam, with a hand-written label saying 'raspberry'. There is a second jar, too, with a label saying 'blackberry'. Inside the blackberry jam jar there is only a tiny bit of jam left. The jar is almost empty.

"We need to send this to the lab," says the inspector, holding it up to the light. "I wonder why the crime scene team didn't take it."

They do not find anything else interesting in the house. The inspector puts the two jars of jam – the full one and the almost empty one – into plastic evidence bags. He writes the date and the time on the bag labels and signs them. Then he asks Sergeant Coleman to run them to the police lab as fast as possible.

"I want to stay in Little Barnswold for a bit longer," he says. "I want to interview the young men who worked for Mark King. He couldn't **burgle houses** and steal heavy furniture on his own, could he?"

"Maybe you need **back-up**," says Miranda. "Maybe you will have to arrest them."

| to burgle a house | in ein Haus einbrechen |
|---|---|
| back-up | *hier*: Unter-stützung |
| constable | Polizist |
| ankle | Knöchel |
| to groan | stöhnen, ächzen |
| twisted | verdreht, verstaucht |
| to grab | greifen, packen |
| fist | Faust |
| jaw | Kiefer |

"Good idea." DI Green takes out his mobile and calls the station.

Two **constables** in uniform arrive half an hour later, and the inspector goes with them to the house of one of the young men on the list. His name is Dean Monroe. The DI knocks on the door. Nobody answers. He tries again. Suddenly he hears a loud noise from the back of the house.

"Wait here," DI Green says to the other officers.

He runs around to the back of the house. There he sees a man sitting in the middle of a flower bed. The man is holding his **ankle** and is **groaning** in pain. DI Green looks up and sees an open window on the second floor.

"Mr Monroe?" asks the inspector.

When the man sees the DI, he stands up. He tries to run, and for a man with a **twisted** ankle, he is surprisingly quick. But the DI also moves fast for a man who loves chocolate cake. He catches Monroe easily and **grabs** his arm. Suddenly, the man swings his **fist** around and hits the inspector in the **jaw**, knocking him to the ground. Monroe starts to run again, but DI Green rolls over and grabs one of the man's legs. He falls over.

"Help!" shouts the inspector. The other officers come running around the side of the house. They grab Monroe, and one of the officers, Constable Harris, pulls out his **handcuffs**. The man **struggles**

| handcuffs *pl* | Handschellen |
| **to struggle** | kämpfen |
| **to manage sth.** | etw. schaffen |
| **to assault** | angreifen |

and shouts, but they **manage** to get the handcuffs on him. The DI is still sitting on the ground, rubbing his jaw.

"You've just **assaulted** a Detective Inspector, you idiot," Constable Harris tells Monroe. "That was a very bad idea."

"We just wanted a little chat, Mr Monroe," says DI Green, standing up. "But trying to run away when police officers knock on the door... well, it makes me think you've done something wrong."

"We'll take him back to the station," says one of the officers.

"This isn't good," Green says. "There are three more men on this list. I can't fight with all of them. We need more officers!"

"I'll organize that," says Constable Harris. "You go and get some ice on that jaw, sir."

---

### Exercise 8: Present Continuous. Setzen Sie die Sätze ins Present Continuous!

1. I drive home.      *I'm driving home.*

2. He eats chocolate cake. _____

3. They fight in the garden. _____

4. We look for the poison. _____

5. They stay in the village. _____

6. You knock on the door. _____

DI Green drives back to Cambridge alone, with his jaw hurting badly. While he drives, he thinks about the pretty little village, **surrounded by** fields and woods. There is even a lit-

| **surrounded by** | umgeben von |
| **to report** | melden, berichten |
| **questioning** | Verhör, Befragung |
| **to pass** | *hier*: geben, reichen |

tle river running through it, right next to the pub. He imagines sitting outside the pub in the summer, having a beer, listening to the birds. Once back in Cambridge  he sees all the people and the grey streets. So many tourists come to the city to see the famous colleges that it is hard to walk the streets in summer.

He parks the car in his reserved parking space at the police station. The afternoon is nearly over but he still has a lot of work to do. He wants to interview Dean Monroe and two of the other men. They are all at the station. The fourth man from the antiques business is not at home, or at his parent's house, and the DI officially **reports** him as 'wanted for **questioning**'. It appears that all of the men have criminal records for burglary.

Once inside the police station, Green finds Sergeant Coleman at her desk.

"How's the jam test going?" he asks her.

"They're doing it as quickly as possible," replies Miranda. "I've told them it's for you."

"And Lydia King? She's still being held for questioning?"

"Both Mrs King and Mr Lowry are in cells," Miranda says, **passing** the inspector the files on them. "Of course, there's a big risk that they'll try to leave the country once we release them."

Bereits seit dem 13. Jahrhundert prägt die Universität mit mittelalterlichen und georgianischen Gebäuden das Stadtbild von **Cambridge**. Dominiert vom Fluss Cam und zahlreichen ehrwürdigen Colleges zieht die Stadt Touristen aus aller Welt an.

"I agree," says DI Green. "I think we'll have to arrest them. Our twenty-four hours is nearly up. The **evidence** is **circumstantial** – the big **inheritance**, the flights to Barbados – but I think it's enough."

"So, you really think they did it?" asks the sergeant.

"I'm not sure," the inspector answers. "But it looks bad. I

| | |
|---|---|
| **circumstantial evidence** | Indizien-beweis |
| **inheritance** | Erbe |
| **legal aid** | Rechtshilfe |
| **lawyer** | Anwalt, Anwältin |
| **sentence** | *hier*: Strafe; Satz |
| **involved** | beteiligt |
| **to charge sb.** | jmd. anklagen |

want to see what comes out of the interviews with King's employees. I'll ask them about Lydia, too."

The DI tries to interview Dean Monroe first. The young man has a **legal aid lawyer** with him in the interview room. Green makes it clear to both of them that Monroe's **sentence** for burglary can be lighter. All he has to do is tell them some details about the business and about the men **involved**. But he won't talk.

"Are you going to **charge me** with something, or let me go home?" Monroe says, angrily.

"Actually," the inspector replies, "I'm charging you with assaulting a police officer. While you think about that, I'll talk to your friends from your job in antiques. I wonder what they'll say about your role in the business."

---

**Exercise 9: Fill in the blanks.** Lesen Sie weiter und setzen Sie die angegebenen Begriffe richtig ein!

information   into   a lot   make   owners

purchase   steal   voice

Suddenly, Monroe finds his **1.** _____. He decides he

wants to **2.** _____ a statement about the stolen antiques, and he also wants to exchange **3.** _____ for a lighter sentence. He tells the inspector that he and the other three men break **4.** _____ houses when the **5.** _____ are away.

"King told us which houses to **6.** _____ from," Monroe says. "Later, he invented **7.** _____ receipts. He paid us quite **8.** _____."

"And Mrs King?" Green asks. "Did she know about the thefts?"
"I don't think so. But I could tell you a lot about her!"
"Like what, for example?" asks the inspector.
Monroe sits back in his chair and crosses his arms. "She'll flirt with anything in trousers. They say she's had dozens of affairs. I'm surprised Mark didn't kill her, not the other way around!"
"Do you think Mrs King killed her husband?" Green asks.
"Everyone in the village is talking about it," the young man replies. "We all know she did it, or some boyfriend of hers did it."

DI Green asks one of the other officers to help Monroe make his statement and leaves him to talk to his lawyer.
He is just on his way to the next interview room, where another young man from the village is waiting, when he spots a coffee machine in someone's office. He can smell the freshly-made coffee. He knocks, but there is nobody inside. He is just about to go in when Sergeant Coleman comes down the corridor.
"If you want some coffee, I can get you some," she says, smiling. "Inspector McGraw won't be happy if you take hers."

"I was just... enjoying the smell," says the inspector.

"Well, I've been looking for you," Miranda says, holding up a piece of paper. "The report on the jam just came through. It tested positive for digoxin."

"I don't think our young antiques thieves put poison in King's jam, do you?" says the inspector. "I don't think it's their style. But I want to talk to Mrs King right now."

"I'll send her to interview room three," the sergeant says. "And I'll make sure there's some coffee waiting for you there."

| | |
|---|---|
| theft | Diebstahl |
| they say | *hier*: es heißt, alle sagen |
| dozen | Dutzend |
| to spot sth. | etw. entdecken |
| thief, thieves *pl* | Dieb(in) |

"And one for Mrs King, too. She's going to need a good explanation for everything, and we could be here all night."

# 4 Interview with a Poisoner

Lydia King looks terrible. There are big dark rings under her eyes. She is not wearing any make-up and her hair **is a mess**. She looks as if she has been crying all night.

DI Green has seen lots of murderers in his career as a police officer, and Mrs King does not look like one. He remembers that Craig Lowry is still a suspect, too. It is possible that Lowry murdered Mark King and Lydia King knew about it. Her lover a murderer, her Barbados plans ruined, and a night in a police cell – no wonder she is crying, Green thinks.

DI Green pulls a chair out and sits down at the table. There are two big **mugs** of coffee and he pushes one over to her. The door opens and Sergeant Cole-man comes in with Mrs King's lawyer. The lawyer sits next to Lydia and asks her if she is okay.

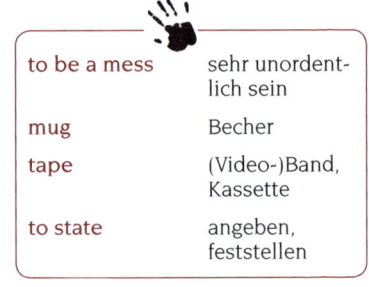

| | |
|---|---|
| to be a mess | sehr unordent-lich sein |
| mug | Becher |
| tape | (Video-)Band, Kassette |
| to state | angeben, feststellen |

"Do I look like I'm okay?" she asks.

Miranda sets up the **tape** to record the interview. She **states** the time and the date and says who is present in the room. Then she sits down next to DI Green.

Now they can start.

"I'm going to get straight to the point," says DI Green. "We've found the jam."

"You didn't tell me about jam," says the lawyer. "If you're going to accuse my client…"

"What jam?" Lydia King interrupts. "What are you talking about, Inspector?"

She is confused and looks from DI Green to Miranda.

Miranda opens one of her files.

"We found a poison called digoxin in your jam. It's not enough to kill anyone, unless you ate a whole jar. But it proves the poison that killed your husband was in your house."

## Exercise 10: Unscramble the sentences. Bringen Sie die Wörter in die richtige Reihenfolge.

1. poison   they   in   found   jam   the   homemade

   _____

2. interviews   the   Monroe   he   burglaries   about

   _____

3. think   you   Mrs King   husband   do   her   killed

   _____

4. purchase   any   find   I   can't   receipts

   _____

5. in   murderers   career   DI Green   seen   many   his   has

   _____

Mrs King looks shocked. "He was poisoned by jam? He ate it nearly every day! My God, I could have died, too. But I never ate it. Too much sugar."

"Where did you get the digoxin?" asks the inspector, sipping his coffee. "Did Lowry give it to you?"

"I didn't do it!" shouts Mrs King, looking at her lawyer. "Tell him I had nothing to do with any jam! The neighbour gave it to us, Ida McBride. The homemade jam, and lots of cakes. Mark ate a big custard tart for afternoon tea on the day he died. I told you that. Ida gave us that custard tart, too!"

The DI and Miranda look at each other.

"Interview over," says Green.

He jumps up and switches off the tape. Miranda grabs her files and they rush out of the room.


Half an hour later, they are in Little Barnswold again. Miranda parks in front of Ida McBride's cottage, right next to the Kings'.

"There's no motive," she says, as she gets out of the car. "Why would an old lady want to kill Mark King?"

"That's what we'll find out," the inspector replies.

"My God! She could be giving jam and custard tarts to everyone in the village!" says Miranda. "I told you village life was scary. You don't get poisoned jam from a nice city supermarket!"

"Hold on," says DI Green, "Didn't Reverend Davies say that Ida was sick? Maybe she's poisoning herself."

Miranda knocks on the door.

Surprisingly, the reverend himself opens it.

"Hello Inspector, Sergeant Coleman. Is everything alright?" he asks.

"We need to speak to Ms McBride," the inspector says.

"Of course," says the reverend, "I've just brought her some chicken soup."

38

In the living room, Ida is sitting on the sofa. She smiles when Green and Miranda walk in. She starts to stand up.

"No, no," says the inspector. "Don't get up. We can talk here in the living room."

"But I must put the kettle on," she says. "I've got scones and a new jar of homemade jam."

Miranda looks at the inspector.

| | |
|---|---|
| ingredient | Zutat |
| rude | grob, unhöflich |

"It's the jam we want to talk about," she tells Ida. "Sorry, Reverend, we'd like to talk to Ida alone."

"Of course," says Reverend Davies, looking worried. "Call me if you need me later, Ida."

"Thank you, Reverend," Ida says as he leaves.

The inspector and Miranda sit down.

"Mrs McBride," DI Green starts. "Did you give Mark King some jam and a custard tart?"

"Yes," she replies, "and some scones and cakes and things. Why?"

"Did you use a special ingredient?" asks DI Green.

"I didn't make them, Inspector!" she says. "Mavis gives them to me."

"Mavis Hammond?"

"She kept giving me things. Homemade jam, cakes, biscuits. When I started to feel sick, I couldn't eat them any more, except for a bit of jam. She kept bringing things and I didn't want to be rude. I couldn't say no, and Mark King loved cakes for his afternoon tea."

"We found poison in the jam," says the inspector.

Ida looks shocked.

"And we suspect that there was so much poison in the custard tart that it killed Mark King," DI Green continues.

He is looking at Ida very seriously.

"Oh, no!" Ida cries out. "Are you sure?"

"The jam made him ill. He already had kidney problems. The custard tart turned a kidney problem into **kidney failure**. That's why we need to get a crime scene team in to search your house. Ida, did you eat any of the jam or cakes yourself?"

"Yes, of course," says Ida. "But lately I've felt too sick. I've had a little bit of the jam on toast, but I've given a lot of the jams and cakes to the Kings."

| | |
|---|---|
| **kidney failure** | Nierenversagen |
| **to remind sb.** | jmd. erinnern (an) |
| **to kneel** | (sich hin)knien |
| **flower bed** | Blumenbeet |

DI Green and Miranda look at each other.

"I'm going to call an ambulance right now," says the inspector. "I suspect you have digoxin poisoning from the jam, Ida. Nausea is one of the symptoms. You need to go to hospital and get tested."

"This is terrible!" Ida says.

Twenty minutes later, DI Green and Sergeant Coleman watch the ambulance drive away from Ida's house.

"**Remind me** to always talk to old ladies first," says the inspector.

"I'll remember, sir," says Miranda.

"Now, let's talk to Mavis Hammond before she can make any more custard tarts!"

"I hope she doesn't make cakes for the church café, too," says Miranda. "You've eaten a few of them, haven't you?"

"Thank you, Sergeant Coleman. That's very helpful."

Mavis lives in a small, white house with a pretty garden. There's no answer at the front door, so they go around to the back. Mavis is there, in a large garden full of flowers. She is wearing a big hat and has a basket with gardening tools next to her. She's **kneeling** in the **flower beds**, but when she sees the police officers, she stands up.

"Hello!" she says. "I thought I heard the doorbell."

"We need to talk to you, Mrs Hammond," says Green.

"Of course," she replies. Then she looks at her flowers. "Aren't they beautiful? Look at those **peonies**. I love summer!"

"Yes," says Miranda. "You have a wonderful garden. It's like something out of a magazine."

"The secret is to put the tall flowers at the back and the shorter ones in front," Mavis says. "Can you see? I've put these white **foxgloves** along the wall, then the pink peonies, then the…"

"Foxgloves," the inspector interrupts.

Miranda looks at him and **frowns**. "Sir?"

| | |
|---|---|
| peony | Pfingstrose |
| foxglove | Fingerhut (Pflanze) |
| to frown | die Stirn runzeln |
| marigold | Ringelblume |

"My favourite flower," says Mavis. "My garden is filled with them. They're so lovely, especially the pink ones."

"And so useful," says DI Green, "for making poison, for example. Digoxin. Of course. Digitalis purpurea, the common foxglove."

"You're right, Inspector," says Mavis. "It's also known as Dead Man's Bells or Witches Gloves. That's what you want to talk about, isn't it? Let's go inside and I'll put the kettle on."

"No," says DI Green. "Let's talk right here. Reverend Davies told me you were a cleaner at the church and Ida was the flower lady there. Then, when Ida got sick, you started doing the flowers."

"Well, yes," agrees Mavis. "I know about flowers, I know what looks best… Some of Ida's flower arrangements were terrible. Once, she used **marigolds**! Can you believe it?"

"So you thought you'd poison Ida and take her job," says the inspector. "She got sick, but not sick enough. The reverend would give her the flower job back as soon as she got better. And you'd be back to cleaning."

"The reverend," says Mavis, "is an idiot."

"How did you do it?" Green asks. "How did you make the poison?"

"It's really quite easy," replies Mavis, taking her hat off. "I take the leaves and the roots from the foxgloves. Then I pour boiling water on them and make an infusion. I add it to the jam and the cakes with lots of sugar. Digitalis is very bitter."

| leaves *pl* | Blätter |
| root | Wurzel |
| infusion | *hier*: Aufguss |
| annoying | ärgerlich, nervig |
| to stab | (er)stechen, ein-stechen auf |
| to pat | tätscheln |
| attempted murder | versuchter Mord |

"And deadly. There was enough digoxin in that custard tart to kill a sick old lady. Or a man with kidney problems."

"What?" asks Mavis. "What man?"

"Mark King," Miranda says. "Did you know that Ida was giving your delicious homemade jams and cakes to her next door neighbour?"

"Mark King?" says Mavis. She looks upset. "I didn't want him to die. I just wondered why the poison didn't kill Ida. It was very annoying."

"Annoying?" Miranda shouts. "You tried to murder an innocent person and you were annoyed?"

"Sergeant, please calm down," DI Green says, putting his hand on her arm.

"Just get me back to the city," says Miranda. "It's better there. Drunk people stab each other outside pubs; they steal things to buy drugs. You know where you are in the city!"

The inspector pats her arm. Then he looks at the old lady.

"Mavis Hammond, I'm arresting you for the attempted murder of Ida McBride and for the death of Mark King."

# A Model Murder

**Oliver Astley**

# A Weekend Away

Juliet Stubbs enters the kitchen and screams with **delight**.

"Oh, George, you remembered!" she cries.

"Of course," replies her husband with a smile, "you **reminded me** every day last week."

"What pretty flowers!" she continues, excited.

Exactly twenty-five years ago, Juliet Sprout married George Stubbs. Today is their silver **wedding anniversary**. Twenty-five white roses are standing in a new crystal vase on the breakfast table. There is also a silver **envelope** next to the teapot. Juliet smells the roses and looks nervously at the envelope.

"Open it," he says, "it won't bite."

His wife picks up a knife and cuts the paper. George turns around and takes some bread from the toaster.

"Bath!" his wife **exclaims**. "I love Bath, it's such a charming city!"

George **raises** his eyebrows. "Keep reading," he says and takes some milk from the fridge.

She **reads aloud** a letter from a five-star hotel and looks at two tickets to the city's famous **Roman Baths**.

| | |
|---|---|
| delight | Freude, Entzücken |
| to remind sb. | jmd. erinnern (an) |
| wedding anniversary | Hochzeitstag |
| envelope | Briefumschlag |
| to exclaim | (aus)rufen |
| to raise sth. | etw. (an)heben; erhöhen |
| to read aloud | laut (vor)lesen |
| Roman Baths *pl* | Römisches Bad |

"What's wrong?" her husband asks when she stops talking.

"It's perfect!" she cries, "Thank you so much. I love you."

They kiss and sit down to eat, listening to the morning

| to grunt | brummeln; grunzen |
| celebrity gossip | Promiklatsch |
| delighted | erfreut, entzückt |
| to enjoy sth. | etw. genießen, Freude haben an etw. |
| ⚡ culture vulture | Kulturfanatiker(in) |

news on the radio. It is not very interesting, but Juliet has something to say about each report between mouthfuls of breakfast. George sits in silence; he sometimes smiles at his wife or **grunts** in agreement, but his food interests him more than political scandal and **celebrity gossip**.

Less than an hour later, they are in the car on their way to Bath. As a police inspector, people imagine that Inspector George Stubbs is an organized man. In fact he is usually the opposite, a chaotic and forgetful person who loses his car keys almost every day. His wife is still surprised that he remembered their wedding anniversary. She is **delighted** that they are going somewhere special to celebrate. They live in Devon, a beautiful part of south west England with low, green hills and wild moors. Although the countryside is full of pretty tourist attractions and peaceful walks, living in the country makes it more difficult to find enough time to visit a city and **enjoy** the culture it has to offer.

**Exercise 1: Adjectives.** Lesen Sie weiter und unterstreichen Sie alle acht Adjektive!

Juliet calls her husband a "**culture vulture**". He loves history, literature, classical music, museums, art and a good bottle of French wine. She usually has to follow him around

**exhibitions** and old bookshops in the city. It is important to spend time together, though. George is always so busy at work these days that it is a **blessing** whenever he has free time. They do everything together, even if she would really prefer to shop for expensive clothes or visit the cinema.

"You can decide what we do today," her husband says when their car is on the motorway. "We can go anywhere you want and do anything you want. You're the boss."

Juliet picks up the tourist brochure for the city of Bath and looks once again at all of the pictures inside. Her husband is a very kind man indeed, she thinks.

"Well, we have to visit Bath Abbey,[i] of course. It's a special day for both of us, and I

> Im Englischen werden Eigennamen und Titel, die als Teil eines Namens verwendet werden, großgeschrieben.
> *The abbey is old.* – Die Abtei ist alt.
> Aber: *Bath Abbey is famous.* – Die Abtei von Bath ist berühmt.

know you've wanted to see it for a long time," she says. "Let's go there first, then we can spend the rest of the afternoon in the shops, go out somewhere **posh** to eat and maybe see a musical tonight, if we can still get our hands on some tickets."

| | |
|---|---|
| exhibition | Ausstellung |
| blessing | Segen |
| abbey | Abtei |
| posh | vornehm, schick |
| to suppose | annehmen, vermuten |

George opens and closes his mouth without saying a word. He puts another sweet in his mouth. "We can just eat at the hotel if it's easier," his wife says.

He laughs and says that anything at all is fine by him.

"It sounds like a long day," he adds, "but I **suppose** we'll get all the **rest** we need in the Roman Baths on Sunday, won't we?"

"Yes, absolutely!" Juliet agrees. She looks through the brochure and finds the page with Bath's most famous **sight**. "I think I could spend all day there. It's a pity they don't let the public

| | |
|---|---|
| rest | *hier*: Ruhe, Pause |
| sight | Sehenswürdigkeit; Anblick |
| thermal spa | Thermalbad |
| to complain | sich beschweren |
| to wave | schwenken; winken |
| at the top of one's voice | aus vollem Hals, mit lauter Stimme |

use the old building, it looks so wonderful. But the new **thermal spa** looks just as beautiful. Have you seen this picture, George?"

"I'm trying to drive, Juliet!" he **complains** when his wife **waves** the brochure in front of his nose. "Yes, I've seen it, and it does look lovely. But please let me get us there alive!"

Juliet laughs and sits back in her seat. One of her favourite songs is just starting. She rolls the window down a little and begins to sing **at the top of her voice**.

---

**Exercise 2: True or false?** Welche der folgenden Aussagen sind wahr? Kreuzen Sie an!

1. It is the Stubbs' golden wedding anniversary.  ❒
2. Juliet opens the envelope with a knife.  ❒
3. George is an organized man.  ❒
4. Mr and Mrs Stubbs have the same interests.  ❒
5. Devon is in south east England.  ❒
6. The abbey is not the most famous sight in Bath.  ❒
7. The Stubbs travel by train.  ❒
8. People can have a bath in the antique Roman Baths.  ❒

| entrance | Eingang |
| tip | *hier*: Trinkgeld |
| crowded | gedrängt, überfüllt |
| enormous | riesig, enorm |
| carving | Schnitzerei |
| impressive | beeindruckend |
| cute | niedlich |

Shortly before midday, George parks in front of the Malvern Hotel. His wife gets out of the car and looks up at the sky, then at the architecture of the building.

"Oh, George," she says quietly, "isn't it a posh hotel!"

"It's very posh," he replies and hands the car keys to the pageboy. Another young man is standing by the main entrance and welcomes the couple to the hotel. Moments later, while they are checking in, the pageboy returns with the Stubbs' car keys and suitcase.

"You are a helpful young man," says Juliet thankfully.

She puts a handful of sweets in his hand instead of a tip. Most guests give him a £2 coin or a £5 note. He smiles politely, turns around and looks unhappy as he puts the sweets into his pocket.

After a short rest and a cup of tea, Mr and Mrs Stubbs leave the hotel and begin their tour of Bath with a visit to the abbey. It is a short walk up Cheap Street under a clear, blue sky. There are a lot of shoppers about, but it is not too crowded. They are soon standing at the enormous West Front, which reminds George of Turner's early painting of the abbey. ⓘ He is silent; even his wife stops talking. They look at the detailed carvings and impressive windows.

"Oh my God, is this a cute church or is this a cute church?" says a loud, American voice that makes George and Juliet both turn around in surprise.

**William Turner** (1775-1851) ist einer der berühmtesten britischen Maler. Als führender Vertreter der Romantik ist er besonders für die ausdrucksstarken Farben und Lichtstimmungen seiner Aquarelle und Ölgemälde bekannt.
Die Westfront von Bath Abbey malte er im Jahre 1796.

The speaker is a tall, blonde woman in a jacket and a short, black skirt. George notices that she has long, **slim** legs and shoes with very high heels. She is attractive, too, he thinks. The woman takes off her sunglasses and walks up to the two statues on either side of the church entrance.

| | |
|---|---|
| slim | schlank |
| incredibly | unglaublich |
| to shrug (one's shoulders) | die Achseln zucken |
| irritated | verärgert, genervt |
| to approach | sich nähern |
| halo | Heiligenschein |
| mood | Laune |
| besides | außerdem |

"Who are these?" she asks, still speaking **incredibly** loudly. George thinks she is talking to herself.

Two well-dressed men then pass Mr and Mrs Stubbs and stand next to the American. They look up and down at the statues, look across at each other and then **shrug**, almost **irritated**.

George **approaches** the three tourists with a smile and explains that St. Peter is on the left, and St. Paul on the right.

"You can see that the sculptor made Paul too large," he continues, "which is why the **halo** is sitting on his head like a dinner plate."

He does not normally talk to strangers, but he is in a good **mood** and decides to share his knowledge. **Besides**, he likes meeting foreigners and has nothing against attractive ladies either.

"This is the third church to be built in this place," George says. All three strangers look at him with interest. "The French pulled down the original church after the invasion in 1066. It was ruined again twice and what you see here is from the early seventeenth century."

The two men begin talking to each other quietly. The woman sees them, rolls her eyes and says something to George.

"I'm sorry?" he says, not listening. He is looking for his wife.

"I said you know a lot about this place. It's impressive."

"Oh, I...," George turns a little red and does not know what to say.

**Exercise 3: Verb forms.** Lesen Sie weiter und setzen Sie die richtige Verbform ein!

His wife [1. return] _____ and **insists** that everybody [2. go] _____ on a tour together.

"Look how well you [3. get] _____ along!" she says.

As a very open woman, Juliet finds it easy [4. introduce] _____ herself and her clever husband while they are waiting for the next tour to start at midday. The American lady is just as talkative and [5. tell] _____ her all about herself and her two friends, Jack and John. They [6. be] _____ all from Los Angeles, California. This **impresses** Juliet very much, who [7. watch] _____ a lot of television programmes from the United States. But she [8. wonder] _____ if Scarlet Rose can be the woman's real name.

"Why, yes, it is!" answers Scarlet. "Rose is my daddy's surname, naturally, but I am called Scarlet because I was such a red baby. My parents say that was a sign. They knew I was going to have a life full of drama and **passion** when I was so loud as a child."

"Only as a child?" asks John. "I think the whole church knows who you are now."

| | |
|---|---|
| to insist | beharren, bestehen auf |
| to impress | beeindrucken |
| passion | Leidenschaft |
| to swear | *hier*: fluchen |
| to pretend | vorgeben, vortäuschen |
| argument | *hier*: Auseinandersetzung, Streit |
| embarrassed | verlegen |
| to be scared of heights | Höhenangst haben |
| pew | Kirchenbank |

Scarlet **swears** at John. Jack is taking photographs and does not seem to notice the angry conversation that follows between them.

Mr and Mrs Stubbs **pretend** not to notice and look closely at some postcards of the building. Juliet is still listening to the **argument**, so says nothing to her husband, who is moving his eyebrows up and down. He is examining carefully some scenes from the Old Testament that are on the windows.

The tour eventually[1] begins. Jack continues to take countless photographs with his large camera; John tries to make funny or interesting comments to Scarlet, but she does not want to hear them. Instead, she speaks endlessly to Mr and Mrs Stubbs. George is **embarrassed** to be in a church with someone who has such a loud voice. His wife, on the other hand, is not very interested in the building. She asks Scarlet a lot of questions and finds out all about her career as a model when she was younger. She has some fascinating stories about her glamorous American lifestyle. They fall to the back of the group because they are so busy talking. Everyone else is walking

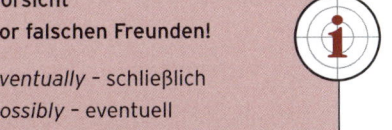

**Vorsicht vor falschen Freunden!**

*eventually* – schließlich
*possibly* – eventuell

*actually* – tatsächlich
*currently* – aktuell

up some steps to the tower, but they decide to stay behind. Scarlet is wearing stilettos and Juliet **is scared of heights**. They sit down together on a **pew** at the back of the hall.

Several minutes later, those on the tour come back down the narrow staircase. George feels someone push his arm and steps aside. A young man wearing a cap pushes past him and then Jack, who almost loses his camera when the young man pushes him away.

"Hey!" says Jack. "Mind where you're going, kid!"

| narrow | eng |
| staircase | Treppe |
| to kneel (down) | (sich hin)knien |
| relief | Erleichterung |
| injured | verletzt |
| nasty | scheußlich; gehässig |

The man is not part of the tour. He seems to be in a hurry to get down from the tower. John is at the front of the line and turns around to see what is happening. The man looks him in the eye with hate and pushes him down the last eight steps. He then runs past Scarlet and Juliet and disappears through the West Front door. The two women run to John, who is lying face down on the stone floor, his head twisted to one side. He does not say anything. Scarlet screams. Jack puts his camera in George's hands and hurries to John. He kneels down by his bleeding face and softly puts a hand on his head.

"Ouch... that hurts!" says John slowly.

Everyone smiles in relief. Luckily, John is not badly injured. His nose is bleeding, but he can stand up and walk. He is in a good mood before too long.

The five do not take part in the end of the tour. Juliet takes her handbag from the pew and puts her hand on Scarlet's arm.

"I'm glad your friend is well," she says. "What a terrible thing to do, pushing someone down the stairs and running away like that."

"I don't think it was an accident," John answers. "He gave me a nasty look before he pushed me."

George raises his eyebrows but says nothing.

"Hmm," says Scarlet, in thought. "Oh! My handbag! My things!"

"I thought you had it," says Juliet. "It wasn't on the pew."

Everybody looks inside and outside the abbey for Scarlet's expensive designer handbag. They ask the **staff** at the abbey and people around the town square, but nobody knows where it is.

"You should **report** it missing to the police," George says. "**I'm afraid** it has probably been stolen."

| staff | Mitarbeiter(team) |
|-------|-------------------|
| to report | melden, berichten; anzeigen |
| I'm afraid | Es tut mir leid, aber … |
| Oh dear! | Meine Güte!; Oje! |
| gently | sanft, zärtlich |

"**Oh dear** – I think you could be right," Scarlet replies. "I forgot all about it when my John was lying on the floor."

She is holding his hand and **gently** kissing his face.

## Exercise 4: Prepositions. Setzen Sie die richtige Präposition ein!

about   to   down   at   of   in   to

1. Scarlet swears _____ John inside the church.
2. Juliet listens _____ their argument.
3. Jack takes a lot of photographs _____ the building.
4. Juliet is not very interested _____ Bath Abbey.
5. A stranger pushes John _____ the stairs.
6. Scarlet forgets _____ her handbag when John is injured.
7. George tells Scarlet to report the theft _____ the police.

"You've both been very kind," says Jack to Mr and Mrs Stubbs, "but I think we should let you go now. We'll go to the police station this afternoon."

Mr and Mrs Stubbs wish them well and begin a four-hour tour of the shops in Bath. George's wife knows

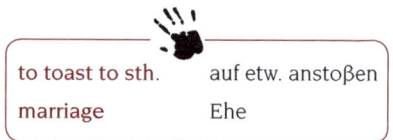

| to toast to sth. | auf etw. anstoβen |
| marriage | Ehe |

exactly where she wants to go and manages to spend a lot of money in the small, old boutiques on York Street and even more money in the city's large shopping centre.

They are tired afterwards, but there is enough time to leave their shopping at the hotel, eat out at an Italian restaurant and go to see a musical at the Theatre Royal at the end of the day. They arrive back at the hotel just before the bar closes and have a glass of whisky each before bed.

"What a lovely day," says Juliet, "and a perfect way to end it!"

They toast to twenty-five years of happy marriage.

# 2 A Mysterious Murder

The next morning, Juliet pulls back the curtain at half past ten. The sun shines on her husband's face and wakes him up. He has no idea it is already so late.

"Don't worry," she says, "we can ask room service to bring us a late breakfast. Today is all about relaxing, remember."

"I know, I know," her husband

| | |
|---|---|
| to be used to sth. | (an) etw. gewöhnt sein |
| plenty | viel, eine Menge |
| impatient | ungeduldig |

replies and puts on his glasses. "I'm not used to waking up so late, though. Did you hear someone shouting in the middle of the night, by the way? Another loud American. I think it was at about two o'clock."

"No, dear," answers Juliet, "I didn't hear anything."

"It was probably one of those two men from yesterday; I'm sure I heard him shout Scarlet's name."

"That's very likely, George, they're staying in this hotel, too. Scarlet told me yesterday. They are visiting Britain, you can see that they have plenty of money, and this is the best hotel in the city."

George raises his eyebrows and says dryly, "Well, I'm only surprised it was him I could hear and not her."

They have a quick look at the Roman Baths after breakfast but are impatient to enjoy the thermal spa. Juliet has an appointment for a massage at two p.m.

| | |
|---|---|
| to treat | behandeln |
| suspicious | verdächtig; misstrauisch |
| body wrap | Ganzkörperpackung |
| That's your loss! | Das ist deine Sache! |
| to wink | zwinkern |

George reads aloud a sign in the pump room: "The people of Bath have used this hot spa water for two thousand years. Its therapeutic qualities **treat** many symptoms. Please feel free to try the water, which contains forty-three minerals and has an unusual taste."

His wife tries the water and looks **suspicious**.

"It tastes horrible," she says.

They change into their bathing costumes and meet outside one of the massage rooms. George arrives first and does not see a tall, blonde lady waving at him. He is almost blind without his glasses. Moments later, his wife arrives and tells him not to be so rude.

"Good afternoon, Ms Rose!" she shouts.

"You will love the massages here!" answers Scarlet. "I'm having another one after you! I want a **body wrap** this time, it's great for the skin!"

"You see," says George to his wife, "it's only women who have them. I'm going for a swim."

"**That's your loss**," she replies. "I can't wait."

Juliet opens the door and gives her name to the masseur inside. He is tall and quite handsome, she thinks. He greets her with a big smile and gives her the most relaxing half hour of her life. Afterwards, her neck and shoulders feel wonderful.

"What strong hands you have!" she says sleepily. "But so gentle!"

"It was just for you," he laughs.

Moments later, she rearranges her bikini and steps into the clear, hot water of the pool with a big smile.

"Can you believe this water contains forty-three minerals?" her husband asks.

He still sounds very enthusiastic about this fact.

"I don't care," she replies, "so long as it feels better than it tastes."

She enjoys the warm water and closes her eyes…

After twenty minutes, Juliet wakes up and sees that she is as red as a tomato.

"Oh!" she shouts. "I have to get out of this water before I cook." Her husband opens one eye and smiles. "Give me another five minutes," he says quietly.

His head then disappears under the water before she can reply.

It is already three o'clock. Juliet is hot and very thirsty; it is time for an afternoon drink. She decides to have a nice, cold shower and wait for her husband. On her way, the tall masseur winks at her and smiles. Suddenly feeling extremely happy, she begins to sing under the shower.

George hears her and feels a little embarrassed. His wife is a loud singer but not a good one. He climbs out of the spa, puts on his **dressing gown** and steps into his flip-flops.

"Excuse me, young man?" he asks the **attendant**. "Which way is the men's changing room?" He cannot read the signs without his glasses.

| | |
|---|---|
| dressing gown | Bademantel |
| attendant | *hier:* Bademeister(in); Aufseher(in) |
| locker | Spind, Schließfach |
| at once | sofort |
| to mist over | (sich) beschlagen |
| to wipe | (ab)wischen |
| confused | verwirrt |
| from head to toe | von Kopf bis Fuß |

"It's the door on the left, sir," says a young lady. "I'll take you."

They enter the changing room and George takes his glasses from their case in the **locker**. "Ah, thank you. Now I can see much better." Just as the attendant is leaving, a loud scream suddenly fills the room. He recognizes the voice **at once**. That was Juliet, his wife! He runs back to the pool and looks for the assistant. He does not notice that the lenses of his glasses are **misting over** and that he is becoming blind again.

"George!" the same voice cries. "It's horrible! Horrible!"

"I thought you were hurt," he says to his wife as she hurries towards him.

She says nothing but takes his arm and pulls. He follows her into the ladies' changing room without realizing where he is going. He slowly **wipes** his glasses on his dressing gown and puts them back on. **Confused**, he raises his eyebrows. The attendant is standing in front of the showers with a mobile phone in her hand. Juliet leads her husband around the corner into the massage area and pulls back a curtain.

A woman is lying on the table covered in a body wrap. That seems normal enough at first, until he sees that she is in fact covered in film **from head to toe**. It does not stop at the woman's neck but is all over her head as well, covering her nose and mouth.

"Dead!" cries Juliet. "Someone has killed her!"

He looks closely at the **victim's** face and raises his eyebrows again, this time in surprise.

"Well, well, well," he says

| | |
|---|---|
| victim | Opfer |
| to murder | (er)morden |
| to question | befragen |
| direction | Richtung |
| to spread | sich verbreiten |
| crowd | Menschenmenge |
| case | Fall; Tasche, Hülle |
| state | Zustand |

slowly, "I know this curly, bright blonde hair. It looks as if someone has **murdered** poor Ms Rose!"

**Exercise 6: Choose the correct alternative.** Lesen Sie weiter und unterstreichen Sie die richtige Variante!

The manager 1. says / tells / questions everybody to leave the pool area and to 2. wait / go / leave in reception. Countless wet, pink legs run in 3. an / one / this **direction** then another while the 4. message / new / news of a murder **spreads** around the Roman Baths. Inspector George Stubbs looks for Jack and John in the **crowd** but can see 5. either / both / neither of Scarlet's friends. He is 6. in / on / at holiday now, but a detective never really stops working.

"It's always someone 7. related / close / unknown to the victim in such **cases**," he says to his wife, who is still in a **state** of shock.

Juliet does not think about what he is saying but agrees anyway. "You know best, dear. **Practice makes perfect**," she says.

After saying those words, she wonders if her masseur could be the killer. Who else was in the massage room?

The police arrive before long and begin asking questions. They take everyone's name and home address and are surprised when an inspector from Devon introduces himself.

"We knew the victim, you see," George adds. "Yes, we spent over an hour with her yesterday. Scarlet Rose."

| | |
|---|---|
| Practice makes perfect. | Übung macht den Meister. |
| modest | bescheiden |
| statement | Aussage, Erklärung |
| curious | neugierig |

"I think we all know who she is!" replies the other inspector. "Any man who has seen 'No Angels in Los Angeles' could tell you who she is. Or at least anyone who was a teenage boy in the 1980s. Sure, it was a bad film with a bad actress, but what legs!"

He winks and becomes professional again, writing down details of the other people present.

"Typical city policeman," George complains to his silent wife.

Scarlet was not the **modest** type, but this information was new. A famous model and a film star. She must have many fans worldwide.

Most people leave the Roman Baths over the next hour. A number of journalists arrive and start asking the remaining visitors questions as they leave. Blue and white police tape surrounds the area. The police do not give a long **statement** to the press, so the journalists are still **curious**; they do not even know the name of the victim.

The inspector returns and introduces himself as Inspector Blunt.

"I didn't touch anything," says Juliet. "I was so **upset** I just screamed and ran for help."

"Neither of us saw anything suspicious," her husband adds. "Do you have any **clues**?"

| | |
|---|---|
| upset | aufgeregt, verärgert |
| clue | Hinweis, Spur |
| evidence | Beweis(e) |
| to confirm | bestätigen |

"I'm sure you know we can't discuss any **evidence**," Inspector Blunt replies. "But I will tell you that the victim was killed not long before you found her. Are you certain you saw nothing unusual?"

"Yes, positive," they both **confirm**.

---

**Exercise 7: Odd one out.** Welches Wort ist das „schwarze Schaf"? Unterstreichen Sie das nicht in die Reihe passende Wort!

1. wonder   think   suspect   know
2. killer   murderer   victim   criminal
3. curious   embarrassed   modest   shy
4. bath   pool   spa   hotel
5. case   contents   box   packet
6. abbey   building   church   chapel
7. similar   related   alike   different
8. question   answer   respond   reply

---

"And do you own a camera that has a case like this?" Inspector Blunt continues.

He shows the Stubbs a black camera case in a plastic bag. George steps forward and raises his eyebrows, curious to take a closer look.

"Well?" asks Inspector Blunt impatiently.

"No, our camera is quite old now and has no case," replies George. "Although I think I've seen one like that **recently**."

George tells Inspector Blunt the story from Bath Abbey. "One of Scarlet's friends has a big camera like that, which is unusual **nowadays**," he says. "His name's Jack. I held his camera for a while yesterday and remember the model. They're not cheap."

| | |
|---|---|
| recently | kürzlich, jüngst |
| nowadays | heutzutage |
| tissue | Papiertaschen-tuch |
| to arrest | verhaften |
| suspect | Verdächtige(r) |

"Do you know where I can speak to him?" the inspector asks.

Inspector Blunt drives the Stubbs back to the hotel, where John and Jack are sitting close together in the reception area.

George and Juliet go upstairs while the inspector interviews the two Americans. John begins to cry very loudly when he hears the news. Jack turns very red and looks uncomfortable.

"Did Scarlet have any enemies?" asks Inspector Blunt.

The two men shake their heads silently and look at each other.

"Were you with her at all today?" the inspector continues.

"Not since❗ breakfast, no," says John. He wipes his tears with a **tissue** and looks at Jack.

"Everybody loved Scarlet," says Jack. "Why would anyone want to kill her? It makes no sense. I still can't believe it's true. Scarlet!"

> **Since** und **for**
> Vorsicht beim Übersetzen von „seit"! Verwenden Sie **since**, um sich auf einen Zeitpunkt zu beziehen, und **for**, wenn es sich um einen Zeitraum handelt.
> *They have been waiting for an hour.* – Sie haben seit einer Stunde gewartet.

The inspector finishes the interview ten minutes later and calls the Stubbs in their room.

He says that he thinks the two Americans need some company. There is no evidence to **arrest** either of them.

**Exercise 8: Fill in the blanks.** Lesen Sie weiter und setzen Sie die Begriffe richtig ein!

puts    crazy    already    both    holding    gives
after    thinks

"He **1.**_____ I killed her!" cries Jack **2.**_____
Inspector Blunt has left.

"Your English cops are **3.**_____," John adds, shaking. "We haven't been with Scarlet all day and he treated us like **suspects**!"

Jack and John are **4.**_____ angry and very upset. They **5.**_____ have four empty glasses in front of them on the table.

"I'm sure he has a lot of formal questions to ask," George replies.

Juliet brings four cups of tea to their table in the reception area and **6.**_____ Jack and John a tissue each. Her husband sees that the two men are **7.**_____ hands and raises his eyebrows at his wife. She follows his eyes and **8.**_____ her hand on the two men's hands.

"I'm so sorry," she says. "We're all sad about Ms Rose. Have you known her for a long time?"

George coughs and drinks some tea. He is thinking about the argument he heard last night and does not want to ask the questions that are on his mind.

"I started her career!" Jack says. "I took the photographs that made her famous. She was on the front cover of four major fashion magazines back in the States. 1985 was our big break."

| | |
|---|---|
| break | *hier*: Durchbruch; Urlaub |
| smoking gun | *hier*: eindeutiger Beweis |
| to whisper | flüstern |

"And you, dear?" Juliet asks John, who is sitting quietly.

"I met her about five years ago," he replies before crying again.

George is listening now and learns that John and Scarlet were like brother and sister.

"I've never loved a woman like I loved Scarlet," John says before leaving to go to the toilet.

There is a short pause in the conversation.

"What you must know," Jack begins, "is that John and Scarlet are both prima donnas. They shout and argue all the time and make a lot of enemies. You probably saw them yesterday outside the abbey. A lot of people think they are married when they meet them."

He laughs at the idea, but his face remains sad.

Then John returns.

"Let's go," he says, sounding irritated. "I need to be alone."

Jack gets up immediately and quickly says goodbye to the Stubbs. Mr and Mrs Stubbs are tired and also want to go back to their room. When he stands up, George notices a ticket under Jack's chair. He picks it up and sees that it is for the Roman Baths and has the same date on it as his own ticket.

"I think I've found our smoking gun!" he whispers to his wife, showing her the ticket. "He was at the Roman Baths today after all."

Juliet cannot believe it. Jack is such a nice man, she thinks.

# 3 No More Clues

The death of Scarlet Rose is the beginning of the end of the Stubbs' weekend break. Juliet is in shock and very upset. She spends two hours on the telephone to her son and then lies down for an evening nap. Meanwhile, her husband calls the police to inform them of the new evidence he found un-

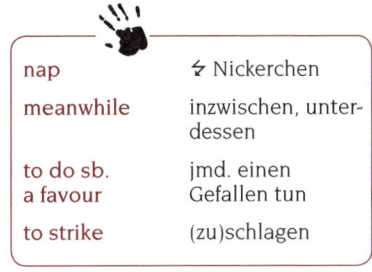

| nap | ⚡ Nickerchen |
| meanwhile | inzwischen, unterdessen |
| to do sb. a favour | jmd. einen Gefallen tun |
| to strike | (zu)schlagen |

der Jack's chair. George feels as if he is back at work. But after spending time with Scarlet, he knows he is very close to the case and is happy to do something to help.

"Good work," says Inspector Blunt. "Could you do me a favour, Inspector Stubbs? Try to get some more information from him. He doesn't know you work for the police, does he? Try to be as natural as you can. He didn't want to talk to me. We need details."

After a couple of hours alone with his wife, George takes a seat in reception and watches the news. Scarlet's death is now in the media. The report repeats all he learnt earlier from the police: they know very little. There are no fingerprints at the scene and of course the Roman Baths do not have security cameras in the changing rooms or massage area where the killer struck. Nobody has a picture of the body.

| to frown | die Stirn runzeln |
| to scratch | kratzen |
| to stare | starren |

The lift doors open in front of him and Jack walks out carrying a black case. He orders a beer at the bar and sits down next to George, who begins to feel angry. Jack does not seem very upset by his friend's death.

"How can you drink beer on a day like today?" George asks.

"I'm scared," says Jack. "Honestly, I need it."

George frowns and scratches his chin. He wonders what is going through Jack's head. And why he had a ticket to the baths.

"This is the worst day of my life, and I should be happy!" Jack answers. He stares at his drink.

They sit in silence. Inspector Stubbs knows that men who drink often tell strangers things they normally wouldn't say. He waits.

**Exercise 9: Choose the correct alternative.** Lesen Sie weiter und unterstreichen Sie die richtige Variante!

"Let me 1. to show / show you something," says Jack after a few minutes.

He takes a new laptop from the black case and opens it on the table. When he 2. enters / entering his password, George sees that he has an expensive ring 3. around / on his left hand.

"These are our photos from London, 4. taken / took last week."

The pictures are almost identical; only the background is different. John is usually 5. on / at the left with his arm around Scarlet, who is smiling at the camera with a professional pose in every photograph. George does not **6.** knows / know what to say.

"They're **7.** nice / nasty pictures," he says. "Happy memories?"

"Happy memories, yeah," replies Jack. He orders two more beers. "Have a beer with me, George. I know you Brits like **8.** one / a good beer."

George drinks for a while with his suspect and finally feels brave enough to ask the question he wants to ask most.

"Where were you this afternoon, anyway?" he asks lightly.

Jack looks up at the ceiling and slowly begins to answer.

"I had a big argument with someone close last night. I wanted to be sure it would never happen again. Can you keep a secret?"

Inspector Stubbs is all ears: is Jack about to confess some-

| brave | mutig |
| to be all ears | ganz Ohr sein |
| to confess | gestehen; beichten |
| trustworthy | vertrauenswürdig |
| ⚡ damned | ⚡ verdammt |

thing? He smiles and says that all Englishmen are trustworthy.

Jack continues to look through the pictures on his laptop.

"Scarlet didn't have many friends, but I was one of them. John is a special friend of mine as well. The problem is that he wanted us both, if you know what I mean."

Jack puts down his beer glass.

"I don't think so, no," says George, confused.

"I mean Scarlet was my friend, not his. But I'm sure she preferred him to me. Even though I made her damned career happen.

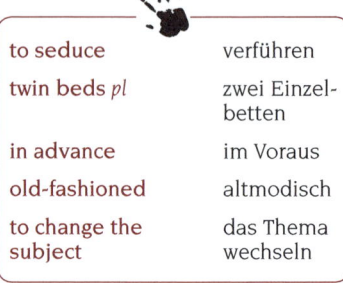

| | |
|---|---|
| to seduce | verführen |
| twin beds *pl* | zwei Einzel-betten |
| in advance | im Voraus |
| old-fashioned | altmodisch |
| to change the subject | das Thema wechseln |

She could **seduce** any man she wanted..."

George recognizes the next pictures as Bath Abbey. He scratches his head and agrees that Scarlet was very attractive. "And very close to John, don't you think?" continues Jack.

"They were having an affair last year. All the magazines had pictures of them in Belize."

"Why aren't they together now?" asks George.

Jack laughs. "Come on, George! John and I are sharing a room here, and it's not **twin beds** in there."

Inspector Stubbs feels embarrassed and says that he understands. "So, where were you this afternoon?" he asks for the second time.

"I spent the whole day here," Jack replies, turning the ring on his finger. "We bought tickets for the Roman Baths **in advance**, but John and I needed to talk about our future. Scarlet wanted to go. She took one of the tickets after losing her handbag yesterday. We stayed here and drank some champagne. John's crazy. We argued all night, and this morning he said we should get married. He even had a ring."

George is an **old-fashioned** man. "Oh," he says. "Married?"

Jack laughs and **changes the subject**. He doesn't want to have this old discussion again.

"Where's your other half?" he asks George.

"Oh, she's taking a nap. She's quite upset," says George quietly.

They talk a little longer while Jack shows more of his photographs. "Your pictures are very impressive," George says. "My camera is old and not very good. I would love to look at the abbey again. Do you think you could give me a copy of the ones you took there?"

"Sure, I'll make you a CD."

George finishes his beer and goes back to his room. His wife is sleeping again with a book in her hands. He sees a police car arriving minutes later from the window and goes back downstairs to open the door.

| smart | *hier*: schick |
| red herring | falsche Fährte |
| witness | Zeuge/Zeugin |
| cling film | Plastikfolie, Frischhalte-folie |
| gloves *pl* | Handschuhe |

Inspector Blunt looks more professional now in a **smart** black suit. He wants to look at the ticket that George found under Jack's chair.

"I think it was a **red herring**," says George. "He's been here all day."

"Really? So he was telling me the truth. His camera is a different model than the one that belongs to the case we found, too," says Inspector Blunt. "We don't know if that case has anything to do with Scarlet's murder anyway. Perhaps it was in that room for weeks."

"What evidence do you have now?"

"Very little, unfortunately," replies Inspector Blunt. "We have a victim but no **witness**, no motive and no more clues."

Inspector Stubbs already knew this. There had been a lot of people at the Roman Baths, but no one had seen anything useful.

"I'm sure you know that fingers usually leave prints on **cling film**," the inspector continues. "In this case, they didn't. The man was wearing **gloves**."

A masseur does not normally wear gloves, George thinks.

"Who works in the massage room where Scarlet was killed?" he asks. "And where was he – or she – at the time of the murder?"

"He was in the office," replies the inspector. "He finished work at two o'clock for lunch and so in theory his room was empty. We have no idea who was in there with Ms Rose because all the other masseurs were with customers. They have an alibi."

"This means you have one person too many," says George slowly. "Yes, the local police **suspect** it was a member of staff from the Roman Baths. They have interviewed everyone who wasn't at work today. How did Scarlet behave yesterday, was she happy?" George explains that she was very lively and confident.

"To be honest, my wife spent more time with her," he says.

At that moment, Juliet appears in the reception hall with another cup of tea and sits down with the two men.

**Exercise 10: Unscramble the sentences.** Bringen Sie die Wörter in die richtige Reihenfolge!

1. to   wants   is   tired   Juliet   sleep   and

   _____

2. a   John   double   with   room   Jack   sharing   is

   _____

3. crimes   the   Scarlet   was   two   victim   of

   _____

4. ticket   useful   not   a   clue   the   is

   _____

5. masseur   when   where   the   was   Scarlet   was   killed

   _____

6. gloves   masseur   normally   not   wear   a   does

   _____

"Are you talking about me?" she asks.

Her husband quickly summarizes the conversation.

"Don't worry," George then explains to the inspector, "Juliet likes to hear about the cases I work on in Devon. She's even **solved** a couple for me."

The two men laugh while Juliet **sips** her tea.

"I had a funny dream," she says suddenly.

The two men look at her and wait for what will come next.

"Someone stole poor Ms Rose's handbag yesterday. And today she was killed in cold blood. That can't be a **coincidence**, can it?"

| to suspect | verdächtigen, einen Verdacht haben |
| to solve | lösen; aufklären |
| to sip | nippen, trinken |
| coincidence | Zufall |
| thief, thieves *pl* | Dieb(in) |
| to shiver | erschauern, zittern |

They all think about this; it is a good point.

"Nobody has found the bag," says Inspector Blunt. "I read a report from the three Americans yesterday. Nobody was able to describe the **thief** in detail. This is quite typical, I think."

George looks at his wife and then looks up at the ceiling.

"Did you say the masseur finished work at two p.m.?" he asks.

George is frowning so deeply that both eyebrows meet above his nose. He looks again at his wife, who is still drinking her tea.

"That's right," Inspector Blunt answers.

"But Juliet's massage was at that time. Who were you with?"

Juliet **shivers**. "I can tell you exactly what he looked like. And his name. That is, he told me his name was Tom."

Inspector Blunt writes down some details and returns to the police station. He appears to be very interested in this new information.

"I don't understand why he wanted to know so much about Tom," says Juliet. "Haven't they already interviewed all of the staff?"

Her husband replies that she is correct, but it is possible that this man, Tom, is not a member of staff.

"But he has magic hands!" she exclaims.

"He also appears to have entered and left the building without being noticed," says George. "A real **magician**."

"But I saw him leave," she answers quickly. "At least I saw him after the massage. He was walking in the opposite direction when I got out of the pool. He winked at me, George!"

George does not say anything in response to this. He thinks about the events at the Roman Baths and asks Juliet more questions.

"But I have told you and the police already," she complains.

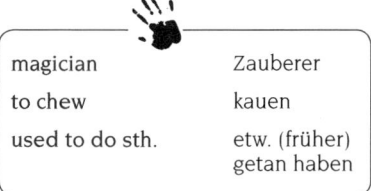

| | |
|---|---|
| magician | Zauberer |
| to chew | kauen |
| used to do sth. | etw. (früher) getan haben |

"When I finished having a shower, I walked past the massage rooms and saw that a door was open. Well, they are normally locked, aren't they? And there was no music playing. I thought the room was empty and went in to look at their oils and creams… and there was poor Scarlet on the table."

Her husband cannot understand how the stranger, Tom, gave her a massage when she had an appointment with someone else.

"It's a busy place, George," she says. "I'm sure it's not organized like a military operation. I just went to the first massage room and I gave my name."

"Well, I wonder if anyone will recognize the man you've described," he says in a suspicious voice.

Mr and Mrs Stubbs pack their suitcase and go to the restaurant for their last meal in Bath. A man is playing the piano and people are happily eating their meals. They do not know, or do not care about the murder that has ruined the Stubbs' weekend away.

"It's a very peaceful evening," says Juliet, "even though we're both feeling scared and tired. Nothing happened to me. Really, I'm fine, George."

Her husband moves his head nervously from side to side, **chewing** his food.

"Don't worry about what didn't happen," his wife continues. "I had a lovely time, apart from the murder this afternoon."

George laughs. It is typical of Juliet to say such things.

"We should be back home by ten," he says. "I need a good night's sleep before work in the morning. Scarlet isn't our problem now."

"I have nothing to do," she replies. "My first student is on Tuesday. But I can do some housework until then; there is a lot to do. I can always practise the piano, too."

Juliet is a piano teacher. She **used to** give concerts, but then she decided to teach because she likes children so much.

# The Invisible Man

The Stubbs return to Devon and watch some television before going to bed. Scarlet's death is on the national news.

Juliet spends the following morning on the computer looking at the pictures of Bath that she took with her husband. Many of them are nice, but the CD Jack made has much clearer photographs on it.

As a professional photographer, Jack has a very good eye for detail; his photographs are interesting to look at. His camera has a very high **resolution** so some of them are much larger than the computer screen. Juliet keeps zooming in and out to look at the sights in Bath again, including parts of the abbey tour that she missed.

Suddenly she becomes quite still. A picture shows a group of people at the top of the tower: George is standing next to John, but there is another face she recognizes. The man is looking away from the rest of the group, but she immediately knows who he is.

| | |
|---|---|
| invisible | unsichtbar |
| resolution | Bildauflösung |
| pale | blass, bleich |
| serious | ernst |
| dimple | Grübchen |

It is a tall, young man with long, dark hair, **pale** skin and brown eyes. He is wearing a cap and looks very **serious**. Juliet remembers that he has straight white teeth and two **dimples** when he smiles.

"Oh, my!" she says to herself, zooming in on the man's face.

It is the man who gave her a massage at the spa. She calls her husband at work for advice.

"Don't you see?" she asks. "If he was at the abbey and at the Roman Baths, it must have been him who stole Scarlet's handbag!"

"That is very likely, yes," says her husband, although he is

| | |
|---|---|
| convinced | überzeugt |
| to gasp | keuchen, nach Luft schnappen |
| The penny drops. | Der Groschen fällt. |
| jealous (of) | eifersüchtig (auf), neidisch (auf) |

not really convinced. "You have found a new clue, at least."

Inspector Stubbs calls the police in Bath to confirm that the two events are linked by the same man. He sends Inspector Blunt an e-mail with the relevant photos from Jack's CD so that they can see the face of their suspect.

"This still doesn't explain what happened to John," George says, thinking aloud. "Why did someone push him down the steps in the abbey?"

"And whoever this Tom is, what possible motive could he have for killing Ms Rose?" asks Inspector Blunt, not really expecting an answer.

George gasps when the penny drops. What did Jack say in the bar when he was getting drunk on beer yesterday evening?

"John had an affair with Scarlet Rose some time last year," he tells Inspector Blunt. "Maybe Tom was jealous of John. Or if Tom had been in a relationship with Scarlet as well, this could be a crime of passion, couldn't it?"

"The American police are already asking us the same questions," the inspector says. "They expect us to arrest someone, but all we have is a name, and now a face."

"At least there is some evidence," says George. "The photograph is a good clue."

"Maybe, but who the devil is that man?" asks Inspector Blunt impatiently. "We can't put his face on television and say we have no idea who he is!"

When George returns to his wife after work, the house looks exactly the same as it did when he left.

"Have you had a busy day?" he asks, smiling.

"Yes, very!" answers his wife. "I've been surfing the Internet."

George **groans**. "Didn't you spend enough money in Bath?" he asks. "Were there more online sales that you couldn't **resist**?"

"George!" says his wife **sternly**. "Be quiet about that."

He is silent and waits for her to continue.

"I've learned a lot about Scarlet to-day," she says. "I **bet** I now know more than you know."

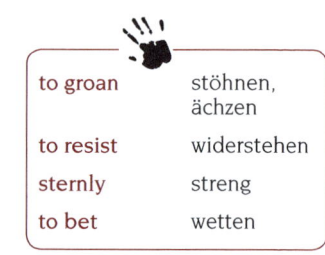

| | |
|---|---|
| to groan | stöhnen, ächzen |
| to resist | widerstehen |
| sternly | streng |
| to bet | wetten |

76

His wife is not often aggressive like this. He raises his eyebrows and looks at her, but she doesn't speak for a moment.

| gay | homosexuell, schwul |
| superficial | oberflächlich |
| headline | Schlagzeile |

"Well?" he asks.

"Did you know there was going to be a 'Still No Angels in Los Angeles'? A sequel to Scarlet's film. Do you remember she made that one in the mid-1980s?"

"I remember," says George, thinking. "Blunt mentioned it the other day, but I've never seen it."

"The sequel was only an idea," Juliet continues, "but Scarlet wanted to do it and was using her Hollywood connections to make sure that it did happen."

"I'm lost," says George. "What do you mean?"

"John is a film director now. He used to be a cameraman. Some people say that Scarlet's affair with him was a planned tactic, a way to get him to make the film. They were together for over half a year, but something went wrong. He ended their relationship. There are still a lot of old magazine stories about it on the Internet. And I read today that he came out about being **gay** at the same time," Juliet quickly tells him and then pauses.

George does not understand the celebrity world very well. He takes off his glasses and scratches his head.

"The magazines made Scarlet look stupid," explains Juliet. "She was in a **superficial** relationship with a gay man. There are much younger and more 'perfect' people than poor Scarlet in Hollywood today. She stopped making the **headlines** a long time ago. People still like her, but she's not big news."

"What about John?" asks her husband. "Are you saying he had a good motive to kill Scarlet?"

"Not at all!" she cries. "And you know that he was with Jack all day on Sunday. But he is a big part in this story."

"So," begins George, "perhaps some people think that John is a **cruel** man. He ended his relationship with Scarlet very publicly and said he would not make the film that was so important to her. This could be a motive for pushing John down the steps in the abbey. Someone does not like him at all."

Two days later, Inspector Stubbs is back at his desk. The phone rings and he recognizes the voice of Inspector Blunt in Bath.
"Listen carefully, Stubbs," he says. "We can't find our man. The photo results are back, but we only have half of the information we need to make an arrest."

| | |
|---|---|
| cruel | grausam |
| to graduate | einen Hochschul-abschluss erwerben |
| degree | *hier*: Hochschul-abschluss; Grad |
| unemployed | arbeitslos |
| current | aktuell |
| record | Aufzeichnung, Aufnahme |
| to live on sth. | von etw. leben |
| pile | Stapel, Haufen |
| land register | Grundbuch |

"What do you know?" asks George. He picks up a pencil and waits, ready to take notes.
"We know who Tom is. His name is Thomas Dorian Baywater. He's thirty-three years old and single. We also know that he **graduated** from Oxford University in 1998 with a **degree** in organic chemistry. The facts don't make sense, though. He's been **unemployed** for the past two years and we have no **current** address. It's strange, Stubbs, the man doesn't exist in our **records**. It looks like he left the country, or maybe he **lives on** a **pile** of cash that he keeps under the mattress. He has no active bank accounts and his name is not on the **land register**."
"How are you going to find him?" asks Inspector Stubbs.
"To be honest, we have no idea."

George goes home in the evening and asks for his wife's help.

"You found a lot of information on the Internet," he says. "Did you see the name Thomas Baywater anywhere?"

"No, dear, I don't think so."

They sit in front of the computer after dinner and Juliet shows her husband the different sites she has visited.

"There are two main websites," she explains. "One is Scarlet's official homepage. It's not very big, but there is a **diary** part where she listed places she was going and others she wanted to visit. The other site is full of pictures from the past twenty-five years. It has a gallery of Scarlet aged fourteen to thirty-eight, as well as

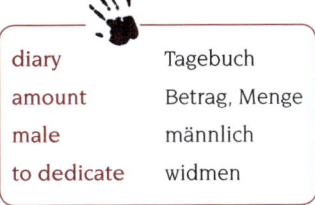

| | |
|---|---|
| **diary** | Tagebuch |
| **amount** | Betrag, Menge |
| **male** | männlich |
| **to dedicate** | widmen |

some earlier photos that her family took before her career began."

George looks at the gallery. "There are over five thousand pictures here!" he exclaims. "Whoever made this website is a real fan."

"It's funny you should say that," his wife replies. "There's a forum as well. Take a look."

George clicks on the link to the forum and begins reading some of the entries from recent days.

"Can you see the moderator's name?" she asks.

George looks carefully but does not really understand what his wife is talking about.

"At the top, George. 'Forum moderator: Mr Scarlet'."

George clicks on the name and looks at a profile with no picture. There is a small **amount** of information. The moderator is **male** and lives in London.

There is also a short biography: "I am Scarlet's biggest fan and **dedicate** this part of the Internet to the most beautiful woman on the planet. Scarlet, I know there will be great chemistry when we finally meet!"

"I wonder what he wrote about Scarlet's death," George thinks aloud. He looks for messages from last Sunday. Many of them appeared around six o'clock when the media made the murder public. Mr Scarlet did not have anything to say until three hours later. The time on his first message is after nine o'clock in the evening.

**Exercise 12: Definitions.** Enträtseln Sie die folgenden Definitionen!

1. the leader of a discussion   _____

2. documents on a computer   _____

3. a collection of pictures   _____

4. someone who is very clever   _____

5. without a job   _____

6. the title of a news article   _____

Juliet reads the message aloud while her husband cleans his glasses: "My friends, today is very sad for us all. The tragedy of Scarlet's death will stay with us forever. We can only hope that she is in a better place than this cruel world."

| | |
|---|---|
| sincere | aufrichtig |
| hoax | Streich, Zeitungsente |

"He sounds sincere, doesn't he?" says George.

The other messages are all similar. "Mr Scarlet" does not say much in them but agrees with other people in the forum who say that they are shocked. One person suggests that Scarlet's death is a hoax.

"Oh, that is very cynical, indeed," says Juliet quietly. "Some people!"

Her husband looks at the gallery again and navigates to the latest pictures of Scarlet in London. Even though they are not official press photos, they look very professional. John and Jack are present in them as well as Scarlet.

"Hmm, I think I need to call our little computer genius," George says.

| | |
|---|---|
| file | Akte; Datei |
| property | *hier*: Eigenschaft; Eigentum |
| to prove | beweisen |
| newsflash | Kurzmeldung |
| to claim | behaupten |
| media stunt | PR-Gag |
| to gain | erlangen; profitieren |
| to cause | verursachen |
| challenge | Herausforderung |
| trap | Falle |

Within a couple of minutes, the Stubbs' son is able to tell them the model of the camera used to take each picture on the website. They think he is a genius, but all he needs to do is right-click on the picture and read the file properties. The model corresponds to the case found in the massage room. It is enough to prove that the killer is the mysterious moderator of the Internet forum.

George registers a profile on Mr Scarlet's website and begins to put his plan into action. He writes a few replies to other people and then writes a message with the title "NEWSFLASH!"

He also claims that Scarlet's death is a hoax. Using the nickname "Truth," George explains that the murder is a media stunt to gain publicity. Scarlet is not big news anymore, he writes, and she plans to "come back from the dead" and cause a media sensation. Minutes later, "Mr Scarlet" replies to the message.

"I could delete sick messages like this, but I will let you have a voice. Why don't you prove what you say?"

This is a challenge, thinks Inspector Stubbs. Mr Scarlet believes it is possible that Scarlet is still alive, it appears. Stubbs has the murderer's interest and hopes he can now lead him into a trap.

**Exercise 13: Verb forms.** Lesen Sie weiter und tragen Sie die richtige Verbform ein!

The conversation [ **1. continue** ] _____ on the forum for the following two days. George [ **2. watch** ] _____ it all the time, but to be on the safe side, he always leaves some time before [ **3. post** ] _____ a reply. Nevertheless, he and Inspector Blunt [ **4. need** ] _____ to solve the case before Scarlet's funeral [ **5. take** ] _____ place in America. Her family are quiet out of respect and do not want to talk to the media at the moment, but there [ **6. be** ] _____ probably _____ press around after the funeral when it [ **7. be** ] _____ obvious that Scarlet [ **8. be** ] _____ really dead.

"I have evidence," writes George in his reply, "and you can see her with your own eyes if you want. She is in Exeter."

The evidence is six photographs that show a woman who looks like Scarlet reading a newspaper with today's date on it. The pictures suggest that she is staying in a hotel in Devon. George then has an idea to make his story more convincing.

He adds some more words at the bottom of his message: "Scarlet made a fool of me once, and I won't let her do it again. If she thinks she can trust her friends, she's wrong! John."

George invites Inspector Blunt to Devon to take part in the plan to catch and arrest the murderer.

The police use the same double from the photographs. She looks very much like the late Scarlet Rose, thinks Inspector Blunt. The woman is

| | |
|---|---|
| funeral | Beerdigung |
| obvious | offensichtlich |
| convincing | überzeugend |
| to make a fool of sb. | jmd. zum Narren halten |
| to trust | (ver)trauen |
| late | *hier*: verstorben |
| surveillance | Überwachung |

wearing sunglasses and a hat so that people do not think she is the model in the news. Inspector Stubbs and Inspector Blunt have the hotel under surveillance with their teams.

The policeman at the entrance sees a man who could be Tom enter the hotel after lunch and informs his colleagues inside.

Inspector Blunt is reading a paper opposite the Scarlet double, and Inspector Stubbs is at the reception desk talking to the hotel staff.

The man looks around and sits down quickly next to the woman. "Scarlet! You're alive!" he whispers. "I thought you were dead!"

The woman is a brilliant actress and behaves very naturally.

"Other people have made the mistake," she says, "I'm not her."

"But I have followed you all day, my love," replies Tom quickly. "I have heard you trying to use a British accent, and I have watched you buying the things you love. I like your new handbag."

The woman smiles and puts a finger on his lips.

"We should talk about this in private, come to my room," she says.

When Tom and the double are at the reception desk, he sees Inspector Stubbs and gasps.

"Have you brought your friend from Bath?" he asks her, looking at George.

The woman pauses and looks at Tom.

| | |
|---|---|
| wig | Perücke |
| to reveal | zum Vorschein bringen, zeigen |
| to reject sb. | jmd. zurückweisen |
| to strangle | erwürgen |
| rage | Wut(anfall), Zorn |

He sees Inspector Stubbs take something metal from his pocket and runs to the door.

"Not so fast!" shouts Inspector Blunt, taking hold of the murderer.

Tom is a taller and younger man, but he is not very strong at all.

"I am arresting you for the murder of Scarlet Rose."

Tom shouts in anger and looks at the double as she takes off her blonde **wig** to **reveal** short, brown hair.

Inspector Blunt calls Inspector Stubbs later that day to give him a summary of Tom's statement.

"Well done again, Stubbs. He has told us everything. He says that she **rejected him** and he **strangled** her in his **rage**. He ran away from the scene in Bath while Scarlet was still moving and must have left his camera case in a hurry."

George is looking at the picture of his wife he keeps on his desk.

"Isn't it incredible what we men will do for a good-looking woman?"

# A Family Affair

Oliver Astley

# Happy New Year!

It is almost midnight. Inspector Edwards knocks on the door and waits. It is the second time that he has visited today.

A tall lady with black, curly hair opens the door.

"Good evening, Inspector. What can I do for you this time?" she asks with a large smile.

"You can tell me the truth, Miss Sharp." He is very serious and does not smile back. "I know you have been lying."

The lady takes a step back.

"Lying?" she asks, shocked.

"Yes, you have lied to me about everything and now it is time to tell the truth," replies the inspector.

He seems to be in a hurry.

"I have no idea what you mean," she says **innocently**.

Inspector Edwards **strokes** his **moustache**. He looks Miss Sharp in the eye and becomes very angry.

"I will tell you exactly what I mean," he says. "You **murdered** Mrs Jones. And you tried to **frame** her husband for the murder. But he didn't kill his wife."

| | |
|---|---|
| **innocently** | unschuldig |
| **to stroke** | streicheln |
| **moustache** | Schnurrbart |
| **to murder** | (er)morden |
| **to frame sb.** | jmd. etw. anhängen |
| **to gasp** | keuchen, nach Luft schnappen |
| **to arrest** | verhaften |

The lady **gasps** in surprise like a bad actress.

"Yes. And now I am here to **arrest** you."

"What an imagination you have, Inspector!" she laughs nervously. "But you have no **evidence** for such a crazy story."
"We have **plenty** of evidence, Miss Sharp!" replies Inspector Edwards angrily. "You were paying Mrs Jones £1,000 every month, almost half of your **salary**. We also know that she had some very interesting information about your private life. Last but not least, you have no alibi for the time of her murder. You lied when you said you were on a business trip. Miss Sharp, you are under arrest. You have the right to remain silent, but anything you do say may be used as evidence against you."

Miss Sharp **nods** her head and suddenly **announces** loudly:
"The bitch **deserved** it! She deserved to die!"

Inspector Edwards takes a pair of pink **handcuffs** from his belt and places them on Miss Sharp's **wrists**.

"And you deserve everything that will happen to you," he says coldly.

| | |
|---|---|
| evidence | Beweis(e) |
| plenty | viel, eine Menge |
| salary | Lohn |
| to nod | nicken |
| to announce | verkünden; ankündigen |
| to deserve | verdienen |
| handcuffs *pl* | Handschellen |
| wrist | Handgelenk |
| to jeer | johlen |

Everybody in the room **jeers** and begins to applaud.
"Boo! Take her to jail!" says one person.
"Go on, Inspector Edwards, lock her up and throw away the key!" a second person adds.
"Off with her head!" shouts another.
"No, that's too quick. Put her in the electric chair!" a fourth person suggests, laughing.
Inspector Edwards – Edward – laughs as well and takes off his moustache.

"The game has ended now. Be nice," he says **sternly** like a schoolteacher. "Well done, Laureen, you made an excellent **villain** as the evil Miss Sharp! I think the handcuffs look good on you, too. And they match the pink socks that I bought you for Christmas."

"That was good fun," Laureen replies. "It's just a pity that I didn't get to murder more of you!"

"Wait until the next **murder mystery party**," says Edward with a smile. "I'm going to have a big event at our hotel in February. I want to have a party for all the single people in town when everyone else is celebrating St. Valentine's Day."

| | |
|---|---|
| **sternly** | streng |
| **villain** | Bösewicht, Schurke |
| **murder mystery party** | Krimispiel |
| **to redecorate** | renovieren |
| **recently** | kürzlich, jüngst |
| **to change one's mind** | es sich anders überlegen |

Edward is Laureen's older brother. They own a country hotel which is being **redecorated** at the moment. There are never many guests in December and January, so they have closed for two months.

"What if I want to spend the evening with my husband?" she asks dryly.

"Nathan? You can bring him as well. He could play the butler. We wouldn't have to pay another waiter then," answers Edward.

The hotel is not making much profit these days. Laureen has argued a lot with her brother about this **recently**. Edward thinks she is losing the business a lot of money. But in fact she works very hard and is always tired. The job is no fun any more for Laureen. She almost sold her half of the business last year to make a new start, but the buyer **changed his mind** at the last minute.

Although he lives alone, Edward's house is always full of relatives at Christmas. This year he decided to throw a murder mystery party to entertain his whole family on New Year's Eve. His large, elegant house **reflects** his old-fashioned taste. Pictures of the royal family and Winston Churchill **line** the hallway from the front door to the kitchen.

His house also has a large library, which is Edward's favourite room. It has two expensive paintings on the walls and over a thousand books that he has never read, as well as many more that he has read.

Ever since reading "Bleak House" as a child, Edward has wanted to live in a **stately home**. His house in Cheltenham, in south-west England, is not as large as the houses in books by Charles Dickens. But it is very **impressive**.

| | |
|---|---|
| to reflect | zeigen, zum Ausdruck bringen |
| to line | säumen |
| stately home | Herrenhaus |
| impressive | beeindruckend |

His guests appear to have enjoyed themselves; they are still making jokes about Laureen in the electric chair.

"Hey! That's enough," Edward tells his family. "It's almost midnight now, and I don't want to start the new year talking about executions!"

"He's right, guys," says Laureen. "Whatever you're doing at midnight on New Year's Eve influences the year you'll have. Let's all have fun."

| | |
|---|---|
| to enjoy sth. | etw. genießen, Freude haben an etw. |
| execution | Hinrichtung |
| ⚡ guys *pl* | Leute |
| ice bucket | Eiskübel |
| to pour | einschenken, schütten |
| acquaintance | Bekannte(r), Bekanntschaft |
| to bring to mind | in Erinnerung rufen |
| to recognize | (wieder) erkennen |

While she is speaking, the music on the radio stops and Big Ben, the famous clock tower in London, appears on the silent TV.

Edward picks up a cold bottle of champagne from the ice bucket and everybody in the living room begins to count backwards.

"Ten, nine, eight…"

A tall man appears at the kitchen window and looks inside.

"…seven, six, five…"

Edward is standing in the doorway with his back to the window and does not notice the figure outside in the rain.

"…four, three, two, one…"

"Happy New Year!" they all shout together happily as fireworks on the television light up the sky above London.

The cork shoots across the room and Edward pours some champagne into long, thin glasses for the whole family. Everyone in the room crosses their arms and holds hands with the person to either side. Just like every other year, they start singing a traditional song:

"Should old acquaintance be forgot and never brought to mind?"

There is a knock at the back door.

"Should old acquaintance be forgot and days of auld lang syne?" everyone sings.

"What does 'auld lang syne' mean?" asks James, Laureen's youngest son.

"It's Scottish. It just means 'old times'," his sister Fiona answers. At fourteen, she is two years younger than James, but she knows a lot more because she listens to her teachers and likes to read.

**Exercise 2: Verb forms.** Lesen Sie weiter und tragen Sie die richtige Verbform ein!

There is a second knock at the door, which Edward **1.** hear _____ this time. His family have now stopped **2.** sing _____ and **3.** toast _____ to the new year. Fiona turns up the dance music that is playing on the radio.

Edward **4.** go _____ into the kitchen **5.** see _____ who is at the door and stands still. He **6.** stop _____ smiling when he **recognizes** the man who **7.** come _____ towards him.

"Simon!" he says, surprised. "What are you doing here?"

"I'm your first-footer, Edward!" he replies in a loud voice.

The first-footer is the first guest to visit a house on New Year's Day. It is often a friend of the family, and a person who brings good luck. But Edward does not know this Scottish tradition. And he does not like it when people arrive at his house without an invitation. So he says nothing.

"What's wrong, old friend? Aren't you going to welcome me in from the rain?" Simon asks politely.

He sounds a little drunk.

Simon McDonald is Edward's neighbour. They do not see each other often because their houses are quite far apart and Simon is a private person. Ed-

| | |
|---|---|
| secretive | geheimnistuerisch |
| cheerfully | fröhlich, heiter |
| to stare | starren |
| coal | Kohle |
| to wink | zwinkern |
| to trust | (ver)trauen |
| to carry on | fortfahren, weitermachen |

ward uses the word "**secretive**" whenever he talks about his neighbour. Simon is certainly not his "old friend". They usually only speak when Simon wants Edward to feed his dog: he is often away for business or on holiday.

In silence Edward watches his drunk neighbour try to walk in a straight line through the kitchen and into the living room.

"Happy new year to you all!" Simon shouts **cheerfully**.

Everyone **stares** at the new guest with great interest. Fiona turns down the music so that they do not have to shout to hear each other.

"Happy new year!" says Laureen. "Is that **coal** in your hand?"

"Yes, it's coal," Simon answers shortly. "That's the tradition, isn't it? And we all know what a traditional young man Edward is."

"That's very thoughtful of you, I'm sure," Edward says. "But it must be a Scottish tradition, Simon. I've never heard of bringing people coal to parties without an invitation. Everyone, this is Simon McDonald, my neighbour. Simon McDonald, this is… everyone."

"Naughty children get coal from Santa instead of presents," says Fiona. "Have you been naughty, Uncle Edward?"

Simon **winks** at Edward and puts the coal in his hand.

Edward does not **trust** Simon, who asks too many questions and never talks about himself. All that he knows for sure is that Simon lived in the area long before he did. He is a very rich and successful Scottish businessman. Edward can still remember Simon's exact words when they first met: "People will do anything for you if you make them think it is good for them as well."

"I thought you were in Scotland over Christmas, Simon," says Edward without much interest.

"I was there for Christmas, yes," he replies. "I needed to come back down during the week, though. Business is business, you know. You don't have a problem with me being here, do you?"

Simon sounds almost dangerous, Edward thinks.

They continue their conversation in the corner of the room while everyone else **carries on** dancing and drinking champagne. Apart from Laureen, who sometimes goes to talk to the two men, everyone forgets that Simon is at the party.

**Exercise 3: Negation.** Verneinen Sie die folgenden Sätze!

1. The party is boring.

   _____

2. Edward is Laureen's younger brother.

   _____

3. Nathan has a job.

   _____

4. The guests drink a lot of beer at midnight.

   _____

5. Edward invited Simon to the party.

   _____

# 2. St. Valentine's Day

Edward enjoys the first weeks of the year. He has a lot of time to relax, but he must also make sure that the hotel is ready to open in February. It should attract many new guests after they have redecorated it, he thinks. Hopefully the business will make a profit again soon.

His only problem is Laureen. She does not help very much during January. They argued again about the business during dinner on New Year's Day when the whole family was around the table.

| to attract | anlocken, anziehen |
| debt | Schulden |
| to snap | *hier*: anschnauzen, blaffen |
| argument | Streit, Auseinandersetzung |

Laureen still wants to sell the business and move away from Cheltenham with her husband and three children, but Edward wants to stay. He said that he cannot afford to buy her half of the hotel. Only an idiot would want to invest in a business that is making no profit.

"You live in a palace with art worth £50,000 on the walls and you say you have no money!" Laureen shouted during the meal.

"I have a lot of debt," Edward replied. "It's not the same. Anyway, you earn as much as 🛈 me."

"But you don't have three children and a husband!" she snapped.

Nathan, her husband, is a very quiet man. He listened to the argument but did not say very much. After losing his job a year ago, he has found it difficult to get work.

In the second week of February, Edward and Laureen drive out to their hotel. The building looks beautiful. They are both excited to see the rooms and spend the day making sure that everything is perfect for the opening on St. Valentine's Day. Edward wanted to open earlier, but it was not possible because of a problem with the lock on the front door.

| staff | Mitarbeiter-(team) |
| bill | Rechnung; Geldschein |

"We're going to be busy on Friday," he tells his sister. "We've had eight more reservations since the weekend. That makes twenty-two guests so far. And maybe some people will come for the murder mystery party if they are in the restaurant during the afternoon."

Laureen wanted to spend Friday night with her husband and a bottle of wine, but Nathan has promised to help at the hotel.

"Edward told me that some of the **staff** have left," he explains to his wife later that day. "They found another job while the hotel was closed. You should have told me. This might lead to a full-time job."

"Why the hell do you want to work there?" she asks angrily. "You know I want to sell the business and leave town!"

"Of course," Nathan replies. "We can leave any time, but it is better to have two salaries than one until then, isn't it?"

Laureen is unhappy about the idea, but she can only agree with him. After Christmas, they have a lot of **bills** and very little money.

> **Vergleiche** im Englischen:
> Zum Ausdruck der Gleichheit nutzt man **as ... as**.
> Dies entspricht dem Deutschen **genauso ... wie**.
> *You earn **as** much **as** me.*
> Ungleichheit wird mit **not as ... as** verdeutlicht:
> *You do **not** earn **as** much **as** me.*
> Unterschiede werden auch mit dem **Komparativ + than** ausgedrückt:
> *Edward is **older than** Laureen.*
> *Simon is **more** successful **than** Edward.*
> Beim negativen Vergleich wird dem Komparativ **not** vorangestellt:
> *Laureen is **not older than** Edward.*

The hotel is very busy on St. Valentine's Day. The restaurant is full of flowers and red balloons shaped like hearts. The reception looks like a room of a real stately home. Edward has put some of his red **leather-bound** books on shelves to decorate the area below the large wooden **staircase**. He has also hung his paintings on the walls so that hotel guests can **admire** them.

At first, Edward was worried that something might happen to his expensive paintings: a drunk guest might ruin them, he said. But Laureen said that they made an excellent impression.

Many people compliment Edward and Laureen on the **posh** hotel and excellent food. As the night grows dark, a heavy storm begins outside.

"How atmospheric!" Edward shouts enthusiastically when he hears the first **rumble of thunder**. "And it's almost time for the murder mystery party!"

"You grew up reading too many books by Agatha Christie," Laureen laughs. "I **suppose** we will

| | |
|---|---|
| leather-bound | in Leder gebunden |
| staircase | Treppe |
| to admire | bewundern |
| posh | vornehm, schick |
| rumble of thunder | Donnergrollen |
| to suppose | annehmen, vermuten |

see Inspector Edwards again tonight. Do you have your moustache?"

"Of course I do," he answers and pulls it out of his pocket. "Voilà!"

Edward then explains the game to almost thirty guests. A murder will take place during the evening and they must work in teams to collect **clues** and identify the killer. Each group plays one character in the story.

"I hope you don't **mind**," he **whispers** to Laureen, "but you're going to die tonight. You were the murderer last time, so it is only fair."

The storm becomes much heavier during the party. **Bolts of lightning flash** across the sky and it begins to rain heavily. A little later, Nathan comes over to the bar. He starts serving drinks to the guests while they discuss who killed Laureen.

"What is it like being dead?" he asks with a smile.

"It is less painful than I thought," Laureen replies. "And I'm sure Edward was happy to see my **throat** cut after all the arguments we've had lately! I hope the blood washes off my pullover."

Some **locals** arrive at the bar to look around and enjoy some drinks. There are not many pubs in the area, so they are pleased to see the hotel open again. They find the murder mystery party a bit silly, but

| clue | Hinweis, Spur |
| to mind sth. | etw. dagegen haben |
| to whisper | flüstern |
| bolt of lightning | Blitz |
| to flash | aufleuchten, blinken |
| throat | Hals |
| locals *pl* | Einheimische |

it has certainly worked. Nobody can remember seeing so many people in the bar.

Edward is happy to welcome them all, apart from a tall, silent man at the back of the group. It is his neighbour, Simon, with a large, satisfied smile on his face.

"Give these men a drink," Edward tells Nathan. "The first one is on the house. They can pay us for the next round."

**Exercise 5: Fill in the blanks.** Lesen Sie weiter und setzen Sie die Begriffe richtig ein!

| lover | turned | later | before | policeman |
|---|---|---|---|---|

| evidence | suddenly |
|---|---|

Just **1.** _____ midnight, the murder **case** is almost solved. The group playing the **2.** _____ has collected some **3.** _____ and wants to arrest Laureen's **jealous 4.** _____. **5.** _____ the music stops and the room turns black. Everybody jeers and asks who **6.** _____ out the lights. A few moments **7.** _____, Edward enters the room with a **lighter** and says, "Don't panic, we often have **power cuts** in the countryside."

Some guests are also using their lighters to see in the dark. Nathan finds some large torches in the office and places them around the room so that people can see better.

The party does not stop: the guests make an arrest and win a bottle of champagne for solving the case. People continue to drink and talk in the bar.

The bad weather does not **improve** as the night grows late, so the locals do not walk home. Without any music,

| | |
|---|---|
| case | Fall; Tasche, Hülle |
| jealous | eifersüchtig, neidisch |
| lighter | Feuerzeug |
| power cut | Stromausfall |
| to improve | besser werden |

everyone can hear the rain rattling the windows and the wind howling down the chimney.

Some time later, the hotel guests feel tired and slowly go to bed. Most of the locals order a taxi and go home, but Simon stays at the bar. Edward notices that he spends a lot of time talking to Nathan and Laureen. He also drinks more glasses of whisky than Edward can count.

"We have one room left if you would like to stay the night, Simon," he suggests. "I'm sure Laureen won't ask you to pay for it."

"How kind of you," says Simon. "Yes, I think I'll stay."

Nathan wakes up early in the morning to prepare breakfast for the hotel guests. He and Laureen stayed in a bedroom above the kitchen last night to get a little sleep before their morning shift. After an extra thirty minutes in bed, Laureen also gets dressed and goes downstairs. She needs to set up the hotel reception.

On her way, she notices an open door on the ground floor. One of the guests must already be awake, she thinks.

| to rattle | klappern, rütteln |
| to howl | heulen |
| chimney | Schornstein |
| shift | Schicht |
| to catch sb.'s eye | jmd. ins Auge fallen |
| bed sheet | Bettuch, Bettlaken |

When she passes the room, she sees someone lying in bed. This is Simon's room; she recognizes his short, grey hair. An unexpected flash catches her eye. There is a knife in the man's back and a pool of blood all over the bed sheets! Laureen cannot believe what she sees. She puts her hand to her mouth in horror and slowly walks towards the body.

Suddenly she stops and thinks twice.

"Oh, very clever, Edward," she says aloud. "Don't you think one of your murder mystery parties is enough?"

Nobody answers.

The hotel is very silent; Laureen has a strange **sensation** in her **stomach**. She walks up to the bed and finds Simon as **pale** as the white sheet he is lying on. His body is stone cold. The whole room is as cold as a fridge because the window is wide open.

| | |
|---|---|
| sensation | *hier*: Empfindung, Gefühl |
| stomach | Bauch, Magen |
| pale | blass, bleich |
| at the top of one's voice | aus vollem Hals, mit lauter Stimme |
| dial tone | Freizeichen |
| suspiciously | verdächtig; misstrauisch |

"Edward!" Laureen screams **at the top of her voice**.

What should she do? Laureen feels ill and begins to panic.

Of course, she must call the police, she thinks.

She picks up the receiver and waits. There is no **dial tone**. She hangs up and tries again. Even though there is still no dial tone, Laureen dials 999. It is useless: the phone line does not work.

As she hurries upstairs to get her mobile phone, Laureen runs into Edward, who almost falls over backwards.

"Did you scream my name?" he asks. "I was coming down to see what all the noise was about."

"Someone has killed Simon! There's a knife in his back!"

"Oh, very funny," Edward says sarcastically. "Don't you think one murder mystery party was enough?"

"Edward, listen!" she snaps. "The phone line isn't working and we need to contact the police. Simon is dead!"

"Are you serious?" he asks **suspiciously**.

"Edward! Go and look for yourself if you don't believe me. He's stone cold dead," she replies dramatically.

Without knowing why, she says the last three words very slowly and in a quieter voice.

"I don't believe you at all," he says. "But if he has made a stupid joke, I'll kill him myself."

Laureen shakes her head and continues upstairs to find her mobile phone. Edward stands at Simon's

to shiver — erschauern, zittern

bedroom door and looks around. He stares at his neighbour's body in silence and shivers. There is nothing he can do. He pulls the door closed so that nobody can enter the room before the police arrive.

---

**Exercise 6: Adjectives and nouns.** Bilden Sie aus dem Adjektiv ein Substantiv!

1. silent _____

2. serious _____

3. dead _____

4. open _____

5. ill _____

6. funny _____

7. angry _____

8. jealous _____

---

When Laureen comes back downstairs, Edward is standing in reception with an open mouth.

"Look what they've done!" he says with wide open eyes. "I can't believe it!"

Laureen finishes talking to the police on her mobile phone. She has been crying a little and looks very tired.

"Someone has stolen my paintings!" Edward tells her.

He sounds both angry and frightened, but Laureen can only think about the dead man. She does not really hear what Edward says. They both go to the kitchen, where Nathan is listening to loud music while he prepares breakfast. The kitchen and restaurant are in a separate building. So Laureen's husband used a different staircase to come downstairs and did not hear any of the shouting.

Edward makes some tea. A hot, strong cup of tea can help them after a shock, he says.

"I can't believe a murder took place in our hotel," Laureen says **flatly**.

"And a **theft**! They've taken my paintings!"

"Really? Oh, that's terrible," she says slowly and pauses. "What else has happened here? Shouldn't we check that everyone else is all right?"

"I think we should leave that to the police," Edward says. "Anyway, the phone system doesn't work. And I don't want to knock on thirty doors to ask our guests if they're still alive. It's only seven o'clock. We'll find out soon enough."

**Exercise 7: Choose the correct alternative. Lesen Sie weiter und unterstreichen Sie die richtige Variante!**

The police **1.** arrive / arrives ten minutes later. Edward, Nathan and Laureen are **2.** every / all by the window and stand up when they see two men in **3.** suits / uniform get out of the car and **approach** the **4.** back / front door.

"Good morning," the first policeman says at the door. "I'm **Constable** Sparrow and this is my colleague, PC Green."

Edward shows the policemen in and offers them **5.** any / some tea.

"Milk and two sugars, please," says PC Sparrow.

"We have to wait for Inspector Hardy to arrive with the **forensics** team," adds PC Green. "But we would like to ask some questions **in the meantime**. You shouldn't have touched **6.** anything / something at all, but if you have already been in the kitchen, I'll have a tea with milk, **7.** none / no sugar. Thank you very much."

The police ask about the **victim** and his relationship to the people at last night's party.

"He's Edward's neighbour," says Laureen helplessly.

PC Sparrow looks at Edward, who is silent, for **confirmation**.

"Yes, he lives – he lived – a little further down the road from me," Edward answers slowly. "He came to the bar with some locals last night. They had a few drinks."

"Do you think anyone else knew he was here?" the same policeman asks.

Edward stops to think for a short moment. "Well, no, I doubt it. He lives alone and all of his family are in Scotland."

| | |
|---|---|
| flatly | flach, platt; ausdruckslos |
| theft | Diebstahl |
| to approach | sich nähern |
| constable | Polizist(in) |
| forensics | Spurensicherung |
| in the meantime | in der Zwischenzeit |
| victim | Opfer |
| confirmation | Bestätigung |
| questioning | Verhör, Befragung |
| to disturb | stören |
| burglar | Einbrecher(in) |

PC Sparrow continues his line of **questioning**: "Did he argue with anyone last night, Mr Vines?"

"I have no idea," Edward replies. "To be honest, we weren't close friends. But I don't think anyone wanted to kill him, Officer. Simon probably **disturbed** the **burglars** and they killed him because he was in their way."

"Was there a **burglary** as well as a murder?" PC Green asks in surprise.

"We found out after making the call," Laureen replies coldly. "It's difficult to notice some things with a dead body at your feet."

Half an hour later, Inspector Hardy enters the hotel. She has seen a lot of buildings like this in the countryside. The usual owners are successful businessmen, footballers or lottery winners.

PC Green quickly introduces his **superior** to Edward, Laureen and Nathan.

"This is Mr Edward Vines, co-owner of the hotel with his sister, Mrs Laureen Casper. And this is her husband, Mr Nathan Casper."

| | |
|---|---|
| burglary | Einbruch |
| superior | Vorgesetzte |
| to examine | untersuchen |
| crime scene | Tatort |
| master key | Hauptschlüssel |
| struggle | Kampf, Streit |
| torn | zerrissen |
| pillow | Kissen, Kopfkissen |

Inspector Hardy nods and does not say more than a short "good morning." Then she asks to **examine** the **crime scene** with her forensics team.

Edward shows them to Simon's room and opens the door with the **master key**. It is the only key that can unlock the bedroom apart from the one that Simon had in his room.

Inspector Hardy asks him to go back to reception and listens to PC Sparrow, who tells her what he has learnt so far. The inspector makes a few notes in a small black book.

It appears that a **struggle** took place in the bedroom: there are objects all over the floor as well as two **torn pillows**, some feathers and a lot of blood.

It is not long before Inspector Hardy leaves her team and returns to the reception area with some further questions.

"I believe you lost some **items** last night, Mr Vines?"

"Yes," he replies, "a couple of very **valuable** paintings. Some papers are missing as well, important hotel documents."

"I see. What else did they take?" she asks.

"I don't know!" Edward replies in a panic. "The hotel is full of nice things. Or it was. I can't see anything else, but losing my paintings is bad enough. They are worth over £50,000!"

Laureen and Edward show the first hotel guests to breakfast. Then they give a list of names and addresses to the police so that they can interview everyone as soon as possible. Most of the guests come down to eat, but six of them are **having a lie-in**.

Inspector Hardy speaks to the rest of the group in the restaurant before they leave. Nobody heard anything during the night. The forensics team must examine the whole building, the Inspector explains. The shocked guests learn that they will have to return home and cannot collect their things from their rooms until the police have finished. This may

| item | Gegenstand, Artikel |
| valuable | wertvoll |
| ⚡ to have a lie-in | ausschlafen |
| complaint | Beschwerde |
| tape | (Video)Band, Kassette |
| power cut | Stromausfall |

take several days. Today, nobody is allowed to return to their room. They are all speechless. But there are understandably no **complaints**: everyone lives in the area and only came for the party last night.

Meanwhile, PC Green asks the two hotel managers for the **tapes** from the security cameras. Laureen gets them from the office, but Edward does not think they will be very useful.

"We had a **power cut** just before midnight," he explains. "There won't be any evidence on them."

"But it looks as if your electricity came on again four hours ago."
PC Green is looking at the time flashing on the video recorder. "It is half past nine now, so that means you had power at 5:30 a.m."

"That's right," Edward replies.

"Any details we know for sure are important, Mr Vines. Besides, many of the houses in this area have security cameras."

"Ah," replies Edward. "Of course. You never know, maybe the burglars came after the power cut was over."

---

**Exercise 8: Prepositions.** Lesen Sie weiter und setzen Sie die richtige Präposition ein!

| in | of (2x) | to | about | at | with |

Once all the guests have left, Inspector Hardy speaks again **1.** _____ the three hotel staff in the kitchen.

"The forensics team will find a lot **2.** _____ evidence for us to work **3.** _____," she begins, "but I would like to talk to you **4.** _____ one fact that I cannot understand. Although the bedroom window was wide open, there appears to be no evidence **5.** _____ a break-in."

"What are you suggesting?" shouts Laureen **6.** _____ shock. "You can't seriously **suspect** that one of us killed Simon!"

Nathan and Edward look **7.** _____ each other in silence. PC Green calmly explains that the police must **consider** every possibility until they have some proof.

"There was a problem with the front door," Edward says. "It didn't lock properly, which is why we couldn't open the hotel earlier."

"But we had it repaired," Nathan continues. "The **locksmith** came out yesterday afternoon."

Everybody walks to the front door to look at the mechanism.

"It's an electric lock," Edward explains. "Our room keys don't open the front door. If our guests want to get in after 11 p.m., they have to ring the bell and wait for someone inside to unlock the door. We can open the door from the office, and we have a monitor that shows the people outside."

"That sounds very good in theory," Inspector Hardy says, "but does this technology work if there's a power cut?"

Edward is silent. Laureen looks at her brother with an angry expression on her face.

| | |
|---|---|
| to suspect | verdächtigen, einen Verdacht haben |
| to consider | überlegen |
| locksmith | Schlosser |
| to shrug (one's shoulders) | die Achseln zucken |
| oversight | Versehen |
| to turn red | rot werden, erröten |

"No, unfortunately it doesn't," she tells the inspector. "If there is no electricity, we have to lock the door the old-fashioned way – with a key."

"And did anyone do that last night?"

"I thought you were going to do it," Edward tells Laureen.

"No, I'm sure you said you would do it," she answers.

They look at each other and then at Nathan, who **shrugs** and says he is only the barman.

One of the managers should have locked the door, he thinks.

"Well, if neither of you did secure the building, it was a very expensive mistake," Inspector Hardy tells them. "And I don't mean your paintings, Mr Vines. This **oversight** could have cost Mr McDonald his life."

She watches Laureen and Edward both **turn red**.

They have nothing else to say at the moment, she thinks, and at the moment there isn't any evidence from the crime scene to link anyone to the murder.

| | |
|---|---|
| to be in touch | sich (wieder) melden |
| for the time being | einstweilen |
| to cancel | absagen |
| insurance company | Versicherungsgesellschaft |

"We have to go back to the station now," she tells them. "Please let us know if you remember any more details about last night. We will **be in touch** again when you can return to the hotel."

**For the time being**, Edward and Laureen must close the hotel again and **cancel** all the reservations for the coming week.

"One more thing, Mr Vines," says PC Green on his way out. "Your **insurance company** won't be very happy to hear that the front door was left open all night."

Edward looks down at his feet and says nothing.

# 3 A Short Investigation

Two days later, Inspector Hardy is in a bad **mood**. A number of questions are difficult to answer in the Simon McDonald case, the murder on St. Valentine's Day.

"We need to consider the facts from every perspective," she tells her team. "Let's look at the two main possibilities. Possibility number one: there was a burglary that went wrong. After all, Vines has **reported** the theft of paintings worth £50,000. Second possibility: there was a murder with a

| | |
|---|---|
| **mood** | Laune |
| **to report** | melden, berichten |
| **thief, thieves** *pl* | Dieb(in) |
| **soundly** | *hier*: fest |

clear motive. I don't know how – or if – the art is connected in this case."

"I have a theory," begins PC Green. "**Thieves** like safety. I believe that any thief with his eye on Edward Vines' paintings would wait until the hotel is empty before trying to take them. The hotel was empty every night before Friday, so why break in with all those people inside?"

"There was a power cut," suggests PC Sparrow. "Maybe the burglar saw that the hotel was dark and thought that it was still empty."

"Perhaps," agrees Inspector Hardy, "or whoever broke in at that time simply hoped that people would be sleeping too **soundly** to notice. There are a lot of 'ifs' here, and I don't like it. Did the burglar know what he or she would find in the hotel? Vines told us that he put the paintings in the reception area **that very day**."

The two police officers wait to see what their superior has to say about the other possibility.

---

**Exercise 9: Choose the correct alternative.** Lesen Sie weiter und unterstreichen Sie die richtige Variante!

"We have no solid evidence to **confirm** that someone **1.** has broken / broke / breaked into the hotel," she begins. "But Simon McDonald's window **2.** was / has been / were wide open," PC Sparrow **objects**. "Even if the front door was locked, someone could have **3.** enter / been entering / entered the building that way and killed the man when he woke up."

"He's right, Ma'am," says PC Green. "That would also explain why someone **4.** has cut / cutted / cut the telephone line. The thief wanted to make sure **5.** if / that / so nobody could **raise the alarm**."

Inspector Hardy holds up her hand and continues to **6.** think / thought / thank aloud: "The front door was left open. The video tapes stop at 11:48 p.m. and don't show us **7.** any thing / anything / something at all that happened during the night. Anything is possible, but we must be able to **prove** it."

"We collected two tapes from nearby houses," begins PC Sparrow. "I watched them both this morning. The houses are both on the same road, one to either side of the hotel. All we can see on the tapes is rain and an occasional car."

"I see. Did you notice the same car twice at a different time?"

"No, Ma'am. All the vehicles passed both houses without stopping, which means they also passed the hotel. But the tapes do tell us something useful," PC Sparrow explains.

"Go on, Constable," she says. "Don't call me 'Ma'am' and get to the point."

| that very day | eben an jenem Tag |
|---|---|
| to confirm | bestätigen |
| to object | einwenden, protestieren |
| to raise the alarm | Alarm schlagen |
| occasional | gelegentlich |
| to prove | beweisen |
| coincidence | Zufall |

"Both recordings are uninterrupted. There was no power cut at either house on Friday night."

"So the cut telephone cable and the power cut were probably the work of the same person," she says. "Or it is an enormous coincidence that both happened on that very night."

"I thought you don't believe in coincidences, Inspector," says PC Sparrow.

"No," replies Inspector Hardy. "I don't. What did you see on the hotel tape just before the power cut, Sparrow?"

The constable explains that he was looking for evidence of what happened during the night. He has not watched the whole recording of Friday evening's murder mystery party.

"That's your next job, then. And take Green with you," she replies. "Four eyes are better than two."

After the two policemen leave her office, Inspector Hardy lights a cigarette and reads through her notes. She needs more information about the victim. A few of Mr McDonald's business **associates** have told her the same details, but she wants to speak again to the family.

There may be a personal motive for murder, she thinks.

| | |
|---|---|
| associate | Geschäftspartner |
| stab wound | Stichwunde |
| file | Akte; Datei |
| handle | Griff |
| to wipe | (ab)wischen |
| to stab | (er)stechen, einstechen auf |

Just as she is about to pick up the receiver, the telephone rings. She recognizes the deep, flat voice of Dr Crab, the pathologist.

The autopsy results are not very surprising. The victim died as the result of three **stab wounds** to the back, one of which went through his left lung. There was a lot of alcohol in his blood but nothing else unusual. The time of death was about 4 a.m.

Inspector Hardy asks for the complete **file** and receives a more detailed report about the crime scene from the forensics team after lunch. She calls her team back to her office to discuss the new evidence.

"What is it, Ma'am?" asks PC Green when he sees the smile on his superior's face. She is not often so cheerful.

"It looks like the boys in the laboratory have found something this time. And don't call me Ma'am."

The crime scene investigators found a few drops of the victim's blood on the window. There was some on the **handle** and a little more on the glass. And someone had tried to **wipe** it off.

"Clearly the murderer opened the window from the inside after **stabbing** McDonald," she says. "He wanted us to think that someone entered the hotel from outside. There is no other explanation."

"It certainly wasn't the victim," agrees PC Sparrow. "Not with a knife in his lung."

**Exercise 10: Simple Past.** Bilden Sie zu folgenden Verben das Simple Past und enträtseln Sie das Lösungswort!

1. write    ☐ _ _ _ _

2. try    _ _ _ ☐ _

3. eat    ☐ _ _

4. speak    ☐ _ _ _ _

5. swear    _ _ ☐ _ _

6. go    _ _ ☐ _

**Lösung:** ☐ ☐ ☐ ☐ ☐ ☐

---

"Which brings me to the next point," says Inspector Hardy. "The knife. What do we already know about the murder weapon?"

"Erm, not very much?" **mumbles** PC Green.

"There are no fingerprints on the knife," she continues, "but we know who it belongs to."

PC Green is looking at Inspector Hardy, waiting for her to say more. She turns to PC Sparrow and invites him to speak.

"I thought it looked like a big kitchen knife when we were at the hotel," he says.

| to mumble | murmeln, brummen |
|---|---|

"Exactly, a kitchen knife," she repeats, "and it came straight out of the hotel kitchen. They have five others that are identical."

PC Green **blinks**. The last murder case took over three months to solve, but things seem to be moving much more quickly in the Simon McDonald case.

"We saw something on the tapes that might be just as important," he replies. "Especially if our **suspects** work at the hotel."

He begins to describe one of the scenes on the tape. Simon was walking along a corridor when he **bumped into** Laureen,

| | |
|---|---|
| to blink | blinzeln |
| suspect | Verdächtige(r) |
| to bump into sb. | mit jmd. zusammenstoβen |
| pile | Stapel, Haufen |
| violent | gewalttätig |
| bank statement | Kontoauszug |

who was carrying a large **pile** of towels. She tried to walk past him, but he blocked her path. After a moment, she put the towels down and spoke to him for some time. Simon then put his hand on Laureen's shoulder and moved closer to her. She tried to get away, but he was too strong and put both hands on her.

"The recording is not crystal clear, Ma'am," continues PC Green, "but it looks like she hit him where it hurts. Then he pulled her hair, said something into her ear and threw her on the ground over the towels. He walked away and left her there. Mr Vines helped her up moments later."

"I see," says Inspector Hardy slowly. "McDonald sounds like a **violent** man. Everyone has described him as kind, but he was drunk, I suppose."

"What about Mrs Casper, Ma'am?" asks PC Sparrow.

"She lied to us. She said that nobody had an argument with McDonald on the night he was murdered. Get me everything you can about that woman," she replies. "I want **bank statements**, credit card bills and telephone bills. I want all the information we can get, and I want it yesterday!"

114

Before the end of the next day, Laureen is standing at her front door face to face with Inspector Hardy. Neither woman blinks.

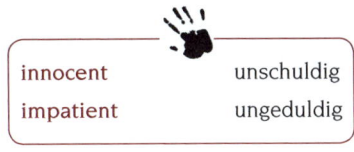

| innocent | unschuldig |
| impatient | ungeduldig |

"You can't arrest me," says Laureen. "I know my rights. You can't have any evidence against me. I'm innocent!"

Inspector Hardy is an impatient woman, but she is polite.

## Exercise 11: Unscramble the sentences. Bringen Sie die Wörter in die richtige Reihenfolge!

1. opened   the   from   inside   the   window   someone

   _____

2. line   the   telephone   cut   someone   outside

   _____

3. was   a   there   only   hotel   power   at   the   cut

   _____

4. shocked   is   to   wife   his   Nathan   see   arrested

   _____

5. weapon   kitchen   the   murder   knife   a   was

   _____

"You can tell me everything at the station, Mrs Casper. I only want to interview you. If you refuse, I will have to arrest you. You're coming with me now whether you like it or not."

| | |
|---|---|
| astonishment | Erstaunen |
| to peek | spähen, gucken |
| ⚡ nosy | neugierig |
| to deny | leugnen |
| dozen | Dutzend |
| disbelief | Fassungslosigkeit, Ungläubigkeit |

"Fine, let's go," she says shortly. "I'll just get my handbag. But I have nothing new to tell you." Her entire family watches in silent **astonishment**. Inspector Hardy takes Laureen away in a police car with flashing blue lights. Some of the neighbours are **peeking** out from behind the curtains to see what is happening. Nathan stares at the **nosy** old lady across the road and closes the door. He cannot believe what has just happened.

Red with anger,[i] Laureen **denies** everything in the interview room.

"Did you ever meet the victim before the night of the murder?" asks Inspector Hardy.

"No. I've told you this before," says Laureen impatiently.

"Yes, you did tell us that. But we didn't have this when we first asked you," she says and

| | |
|---|---|
| Farben sind oft Bestandteil feststehender Ausdrücke: | |
| *green with envy* | gelb vor Neid |
| *to go blue in the face* | blau anlaufen; sehr sauer sein |
| *white as a sheet* | kreidebleich |
| *to prove that black is white* | das Gegenteil beweisen |
| *to catch sb. red-handed* | jmd. auf frischer Tat ertappen |

puts a telephone bill on the desk. "The information that we have marked red are calls from Mr McDonald's house to your mobile. As you can see, some are up to twenty minutes long."

There are a **dozen** calls all together, all of which were made between October and December. Laureen looks at the piece of paper in **disbelief**.

"Who gave you this rubbish? I've never spoken to him for that long," she says angrily.

Inspector Hardy moves closer to Laureen over the table.

"What did you just say?" she asks slowly.

| | |
|---|---|
| statement | Aussage, Erklärung |
| obviously | offensichtlich |
| lawyer | Anwalt |

Laureen thinks and repeats what she meant to say: "I have never spoken to him, I mean. Not really. He was Edward's neighbour, so I saw him at my brother's house from time to time."

"You need to tell us everything, Mrs Casper. When did you speak to Mr McDonald before St. Valentine's Day?"

Laureen pauses for a moment and thinks carefully about what she should say.

"We almost did some business once. Simon showed an interest in buying my half of the hotel but nothing ever came of it. I have no idea why, before you ask."

Inspector Hardy wonders why she did not mention this earlier if she has nothing to hide.

"You told us at the hotel that you didn't see Mr McDonald have any arguments on the night of the murder," PC Sparrow continues. "Perhaps you would like to think about that statement again now that we have seen the security videos."

Laureen does not answer. She shakes her head and is obviously worried. She will not say anything else without a lawyer.

PC Green enters the room during the pause in the conversation that follows and asks to speak to Inspector Hardy in private.

"Casper must have a motive as well. You can see how often she spoke to McDonald, so why is she denying all of those phone calls?" Inspector Hardy asks him before he can share his news.

"There's something else you should know," PC Green says quietly.

"What is it, Green?" she asks impatiently.

"It's her bank statements, Ma'am. She was regularly **transferring** small amounts of money to an investment company in Scotland

| | |
|---|---|
| to transfer | *hier*: überweisen, übertragen |
| to collapse | zusammen- brechen |
| revenge | Rache |
| to admit | zugeben |

for over two years. Guess who the owner was!"

"I'm sure you're going to tell me," she says flatly.

"Simon McDonald! And she lost over £10,000 when the company **collapsed** three months ago."

Inspector Hardy looks at Laureen through the window and shakes her head.

"Do you think she killed him for **revenge**?" she asks.

PC Green nods slowly. "She must be guilty with so much evidence against her, don't you think, Ma'am?"

"She still won't **admit** that she took her brother's paintings for some reason," Inspector Hardy continues. "But yes, I think it's quite obvious that she tried to make the whole thing look like a burglary."

**Exercise 12: In other words.** Welches Verb passt zu welcher Definition? Ordnen Sie zu!

1. ☐ disagree
2. ☐ look at quickly
3. ☐ say sharply
4. ☐ say unhappily
5. ☐ look at for a long time
6. ☐ express dissatisfaction

a) peek
b) snap
c) stare
d) object
e) complain
f) groan

# 4 The Missing Paintings

It is early March. Laureen has been **charged** with theft and the murder of Simon McDonald. She is waiting for her case to go to **court**. Nathan and Edward both visit her in prison and listen to her story **sympathetically**. When her brother leaves to go to the toilet, she speaks very quickly to her husband.

"You have to listen, Nathan," she begins. "The police think I stole my brother's paintings to make Simon's death look like a burglary. I think Edward knows I was taking money from our business. He told the inspector that I made him put the paintings in the hotel. So they are sure it was me who took them. I need you to find out if he knows. Maybe he is trying to frame me! I've told the police, but they don't believe me!"

| | |
|---|---|
| to charge sb. (with sth.) | jmd. (wegen etw.) anklagen |
| court | Gericht; Hof |
| sympathetically | mitfühlend, verständnisvoll |
| to complain | sich beschweren |

Nathan is shocked to hear that his wife is a thief. He had no idea that she was taking money from the company. But he cannot ask any of the questions he wants to because Edward is already returning. He stares at his wife with large eyes.

"You can't keep an innocent person in prison," Laureen **complains** to PC Sparrow when she is back in her cell. "Why haven't you found the missing paintings yet? If you find them, you'll finally see that I had nothing to do with the burglary."

"We don't know if we'll ever find the paintings, Mrs Casper," he replies. "But we find more information that connects you with the victim every day."

As Laureen learns in yet another interview with Inspector Hardy that afternoon, the police have discovered that she tried to sell her half of the hotel to Simon McDonald over a year ago.

"His sister told us that he changed his mind at the last minute, but she doesn't know why," the

| to swear | schwören; fluchen |
| no matter | egal |
| agreement | *hier*: Abmachung; Zustimmung |
| to confess | gestehen; beichten |
| sleeping partner | stiller Teilhaber |

inspector explains. "Apparently Simon McDonald said that he would still help you to make some money, but that you needed more capital to invest."

It was the right thing to do at the time, or so Laureen had thought back then. Edward was rich and single, but she needed the money for her family.

"I was going to pay the business back, I **swear**," Laureen tells the inspector. "As soon as I could. I just needed to wait for the money to grow a little…"

"Why have you kept quiet about your business with Mr McDonald, Mrs Casper? Why didn't you tell us straight away?" asks Inspector Hardy impatiently.

Laureen turns red and decides that it is time to explain everything, **no matter** who it hurts.

"I really wanted to sell my part of the hotel," she says. "One of Simon's associates offered me a lower price at the end of the year. He didn't want the hotel, but I think he knew that Simon did. I was quite close to the man… very close. Maybe he wanted to help me. But I couldn't discuss it with Edward; we had just closed the hotel to have it redecorated. He wanted to forget about the business until the new year. It would kill him to work with a more successful man."

"Did you talk to Mr McDonald about this on New Year's Eve?" asks Inspector Hardy. "Or make an **agreement** with him around that time?"

---

**Exercise 13: Translation.** Übersetzen Sie die Aussagen ins Englische!

1. Laureens Bruder besucht sie im Gefängnis.

   _____

2. Ich hatte nichts mit dem Einbruch zu tun.

   _____

3. Laureen unterschrieb einen Vertrag.

   _____

4. Er hat das Hotel zu einem günstigen Preis gekauft.

   _____

5. Edward weiß nichts von der Abmachung.

   _____

---

Laureen **confesses** that she signed a contract with a **sleeping partner** in December. One of Simon's companies agreed to buy Laureen's half of the hotel at a cheap price on the condition that she continued to run the business with her brother for another twelve months. Edward must not [i] know what was hap-

| Vorsicht mit **must** bzw. **must not**: | |
|---|---|
| _he **must** know_ | er **muss** wissen |
| _he **must not** know_ | er **darf nicht** wissen |
| _he **does not** have to know_ | er **muss nicht** wissen |

pening, that was part of the deal. The first payment would be in March. Laureen tells Inspector Hardy where she can find the papers that prove this agreement. She has hidden them inside a large book in her attic.

| attic | Dachboden |
| to jump | *hier*: zusammenzucken |
| circumstantial evidence | Indizienbeweis |
| to scratch | kratzen |

PC Sparrow and PC Green are both called to Inspector Hardy's office that afternoon. They learn that she no longer believes that Laureen has a motive for killing Simon McDonald.

"She has explained what we saw on the video," Inspector Hardy tells her team. "McDonald asked her to introduce Vines to his new business partner – himself. She called him a drunken idiot and this led to a lot of swearing and the fight we have on tape. I think she wanted to keep things quiet for a year."

"But someone must have hated Mr McDonald enough to kill him," PC Sparrow says. "Who?"

Later that day, Edward is sitting in his large leather chair listening to music. With an open bottle of strong red wine, he is reading through some bank statements for the past twelve months. Things have to get better this year, he thinks.

He jumps in surprise when the doorbell rings, and the first sixteen notes of "God Save the Queen" ring through the hallway.

He is shocked to see Inspector Hardy and two policemen at his door.

"Do come in," he says politely. "Tea? Coffee? Vodka martini?"

"We just want to talk to you, Mr Vines," says Inspector Hardy.

Edward laughs nervously and shows the three visitors to his living room, where they sit down on his large leather sofa beneath a large painting of Princess Diana.

After a few moments, he asks what is happening with his sister's case. Inspector Hardy explains that Laureen did indeed appear guilty, but that all of the evidence was circumstantial. Edward sits quietly and listens very carefully.

"I have some questions about your neighbour's telephone bill," she continues. "Someone made a number of calls to your sister from Mr McDonald's home phone. The funny thing is that we were finally able to speak to more of the victim's family this week. We know that he was out of town when at least three of those calls were made."

Edward begins to feel uncomfortable.

"I'm not sure what you're trying to say," he begins.

"Don't you have a key to Mr McDonald's house, Mr Vines?"

"Of course, I used to ⓘ feed his dog," Edward replies. "But I haven't done that at all this year."

PC Sparrow nods and writes something in his notebook. The last call was made on December 28.

"Why haven't you fed the dog this year, Mr Vines? You told us before that you did this almost every week."

Edward looks out of the window and scratches his nose.

"Ah, yes," says Inspector Hardy. "Mr McDonald's sister received a call from her brother on New Year's Day. You two had a serious argument the night before, it seems."

Edward blinks and snaps at the inspector.

"Of course I argued with him! Do you think I wouldn't notice that my own sister was stealing money from our company? I knew all about it. She took our profit little by little and handed it over to Simon on a plate.

> **Used to** drückt abgeschlossene Handlungen und Zustände in der Vergangenheit aus. Man kann es mit „früher" oder „damals" übersetzen.
> **Used to** wird immer mit einem Infinitiv kombiniert:
> *I used to feed   Ich fütterte früher
> his dog.*              seinen Hund.

123

Stealing is bad enough. But she was giving it to that **bully** of a man! He and I decided to end our friendship at the end of the year when I found out that he had lost Laureen's money. My money, that is. Oh, he was so happy about it all. He said he would own my hotel and my house before the next year was over."

| | |
|---|---|
| bully | Rüpel |
| rather | *hier*: lieber |
| soul | Seele |
| to betray | verraten |
| humiliating | demütigend, erniedrigend |

"It wasn't just a question of money though, was it, Mr Vines?" asks Inspector Hardy. "You heard some bad news at the hotel on St. Valentine's Day."

Edward stares at the inspector, who obviously knows more than she is telling him.

"I would **rather** sell my **soul** to the devil than work with – or for – a man like that," he says coldly. "How could Laureen be so heartless and sell half of my hotel to him?"

"Do you admit that you heard the conversation between Mr McDonald and your sister that evening?" Inspector Hardy asks.

"I heard it, yes, and I saw it," he replies coldly.

The sound of a woman crying at the door makes Edward stop speaking. He turns to see Laureen standing at the open door. She is in tears.

"But you framed me, Edward! You told the police that I made you put your paintings in the hotel. And you didn't tell them that you made those calls from Simon's house just to give him a bigger telephone bill. How could you do that to your own sister?"

Edward drinks the last of his wine and looks her in the eye.

"You stole from me, little sister. You **betrayed** me! And you wanted me to work for Simon! How **humiliating**. It probably wouldn't have taken long for him to ruin my business completely and buy the land for himself."

Laureen looks at him in disbelief. "But Edward – you killed a man!"

"I killed a monster," he replies. "Not that you are much better.

| | |
|---|---|
| rage | Wut(anfall), Zorn |
| to kill two birds with one stone | zwei Fliegen mit einer Klappe schlagen |

I saw what you were doing to our business very clearly. And you didn't need the money as badly as you say."

Laureen continues to cry. Edward tells her that investing stolen money is not the same as using it to buy food and pay bills.

"Yes, I caused the power cut and killed Simon out of rage. It was easy to make it look like a burglary. But later, when I saw the evidence against you, I thought: why not kill two birds with one stone?"


Inspector Hardy has heard enough. She begins to understand this case, but there is obviously more to find out about the relationship between the victim and the murderer, she thinks.

"You will be pleased to hear that we discovered your paintings today, Mr Vines," says Inspector Hardy. "They are safe and in good condition."

Edward slowly scratches his head and nods at the police. He hid the pictures very carefully under some floorboards in the hotel and did not expect anyone to find them.

"Edward Vines, I am arresting you for the murder of Simon McDonald. Anything..."

"I know the routine," he says, almost bored. "You don't have to play Miss Marple."

**Final Test**

**Answers**

**Glossary**

**List of Exercises**

 # Final Test

## Exercise 1: Unscramble the words. Enträtseln Sie die fehlenden Wörter!

1. Laureen `cipks pu` _____ the telephone.

2. There is no `alid neot` _____.

3. She goes upstairs to find her `libemo hopen` _____

   _____.

4. "I must `lacl` _____ the police," she thinks.

5. She cannot understand why the hotel `enli` _____ does not work.

6. Laureen `slida` _____ 999 and reports the murder.

## Exercise 2: Short answers. Bilden Sie die verneinte Kurzform!

1. I can _____

2. I will _____

3. I do _____

4. you are _____

5. we could _____

6. it is _____

**Exercise 3: Reading comprehension.** Beantworten Sie die Fragen zu "A Model Murder" in ganzen Sätzen!

1. Why do the Stubbs go to Bath for the weekend?

_____

2. What is Jack's profession?

_____

3. What does George hear during the night at the hotel?

_____

4. Was there ever a sequel to "No Angels in Los Angeles"?

_____

5. How does Juliet find out what the killer looks like?

_____

6. Why does Tom travel to Exeter?

_____


**Exercise 4: True or false?** Welche Aussagen zu "A Family Affair" sind richtig? Kreuzen Sie an!

1. Edward and Laureen's hotel is closed in January. ❏
2. Edward had invited Simon to the St. Valentine's party. ❏
3. Laureen calls the police from the hotel telephone. ❏
4. The window in Simon's room is closed. ❏
5. Before he was killed, Simon argued with Laureen. ❏
6. Edward found out that Simon had bought the hotel. ❏

**Exercise 5: Translation.** Übersetzen Sie die folgenden Sätze ins Englische!

1. Scarlet ist groß und hat blonde, lockige Haare.

   _____

2. George spricht Fremde nicht oft an.

   _____

3. Es fällt Juliet leicht, Freundschaften zu schließen.

   _____

4. Der Killer schlug im Massageraum zu.

   _____

5. Die Fototasche ist ein wichtiger Hinweis.

   _____

6. Der Sohn der Stubbs kennt sich mit Computern gut aus.

   _____

**Exercise 6: Simple Past.** Wie heißt das Simple Past der folgenden Verben?

| | | | |
|---|---|---|---|
| 1. bet | _____ | 7. speak | _____ |
| 2. bring | _____ | 8. catch | _____ |
| 3. go | _____ | 9. strike | _____ |
| 4. swear | _____ | 10. spread | _____ |
| 5. keep | _____ | 11. worry | _____ |
| 6. leave | _____ | 12. hit | _____ |

**Exercise 7: Choose the correct alternative.** Welcher Satz ist grammatikalisch korrekt? Kreuzen Sie an!

1. **a)** ☐ I don't can fight with all of them.
   **b)** ☐ I can't fight with all of them.

2. **a)** ☐ I want go back to Cambridge now.
   **b)** ☐ I will go back to Cambridge now.

3. **a)** ☐ Let's meet each other tomorrow.
   **b)** ☐ Let's meet us tomorrow.

4. **a)** ☐ He has done something wrong.
   **b)** ☐ He has done anything wrong.

5. **a)** ☐ Please say me what happened.
   **b)** ☐ Please tell me what happened.

6. **a)** ☐ I'd like a coffee and a scone, please.
   **b)** ☐ I like a coffee and a scone, please.

**Exercise 8: Phrasal Verbs.** Setzen Sie die Phrasal Verbs richtig zusammen!

1. ☐ find          **a)** away
2. ☐ talk          **b)** towards
3. ☐ search        **c)** about
4. ☐ walk          **d)** up
5. ☐ sit           **e)** for
6. ☐ drive         **f)** out
7. ☐ pick          **g)** down

**Exercise 9: Prepositions.** Setzen Sie die fehlende Präposition ein!

1. I bumped _____ him on the stairs.

2. You have been on the phone for too long, hang _____ now.

3. We need to speak _____ him about something important.

4. Bolts of lightning flash _____ the sky.

5. There is no evidence _____ a break-in.

6. Where is my key? I've looked _____ it every-where.

7. Edward read the document _____ disbelief.


**Exercise 10: Plural.** Bilden Sie die korrekte Pluralform der Begriffe!

1. detail _____

2. policy _____

3. spinach _____

4. woman _____

5. holiday _____

6. icing _____

7. man _____

8. employee _____

9. address _____

10. information _____

 **Answers**

## Murder at Teatime

**Exercise 1:**   1. made 2. had 3. put 4. felt 5. ate 6. did

**Exercise 2:**   1. What did you eat?
2. Where did you go?
3. Why did you call?
4. Who did you meet?
5. How did you get here?
6. When did you go there?

**Exercise 3:**   1. pretty 2. through 3. flowers 4. case
5. perhaps 6. can 7. jam

**Exercise 4:**   1. He didn't buy two tables. 2. She isn't having an affair with him. 3. You haven't got a criminal record. 4. I won't listen to you. 5. The inspector doesn't eat his scone.

**Exercise 5:**   1. have 2. lying 3. talked 4. makes 5. something
6. need to 7. asking 8. will

**Exercise 6:**   1. up 2. from 3. down 4. to 5. on 6. into 7. on

**Exercise 7:**   1. lovely 2. fresh 3. grey 4. hungry 5. big
6. expensive 7. shiny 8. large 9. antique
10. beautiful 11. small 12. wonderful

**Exercise 8:**   1. I'm driving home.
2. He's eating chocolate cake.
3. They're fighting in the garden.
4. We're looking for the poison.

5. They're staying in the village.
6. You're knocking on the door.

**Exercise 9:** 1. voice 2. make 3. information 4. into
5. owners 6. steal 7. purchase 8. a lot

**Exercise 10:** 1. They found poison in the homemade jam.
2. He interviews Monroe about the burglaries.
3. Do you think Mrs King killed her husband?
4. I can't find any purchase receipts.
5. DI Green has seen many murderers in his career.

# A Model Murder

**Exercise 1:** 1. classical 2. good 3. French 4. old 5. important 6. busy 7. free 8. expensive

**Exercise 2:** 1. false 2. true 3. false 4. false 5. false 6. true 7. false 8. false

**Exercise 3:** 1. returns 2. goes 3. are getting 4. to introduce 5. tells 6. are 7. watches 8. wonders

**Exercise 4:** 1. at 2. to 3. of 4. in 5. down 6. about 7. to

**Exercise 5:** 1. complain 2. curtain 3. nasty 4. posh
5. passion 6. gossip 7. raise
**Lösung:** massage

**Exercise 6:** 1. tells 2. wait 3. one 4. news 5. neither 6. on 7. close

**Exercise 7:** 1. know 2. victim 3. curious 4. hotel 5. contents 6. building 7. different 8. question

**Exercise 8:** 1. thinks 2. after 3. crazy 4. both 5. already 6. gives 7. holding 8. puts

**Exercise 9:**  1. show 2. enters 3. on 4. taken 5. on 6. know
7. nice 8. a

**Exercise 10:**  1. Juliet is tired and wants to sleep.
2. Jack is sharing a double room with John.
3. Scarlet was the victim of two crimes.
4. The ticket is not a useful clue.
5. Where was the masseur when Scarlet was killed?
6. A masseur does not normally wear gloves.

**Exercise 11:**  1. No, Tom does not work at the Roman Baths.
2. Juliet saw Tom after the murder.
3. No, George does not plan to solve the crime.
4. No, the police do not know where Tom is.
5. No, but he thinks it is likely.

**Exercise 12:**  1. moderator 2. files 3. gallery 4. genius
5. unemployed 6. headline

**Exercise 13:**  1. continues 2. watches 3. posting 4. need
5. takes 6. will ... be 7. will be 8. is

# A Family Affair

**Exercise 1:**  1. false 2. true 3. true 4. true 5. false 6. false
7. true

**Exercise 2:**  1. hears 2. singing 3. are toasting 4. goes 5. to
see 6. stops 7. is coming

**Exercise 3:**  1. The party is not boring.
2. Edward is not Laureen's younger brother.
3. Nathan does not have a job.
4. The guests do not drink a lot of beer at midnight.
5. Edward did not invite Simon to the party.

**Exercise 4:** 1. is 2. is 3. looks 4. has put 5. to decorate
6. has hung 7. can 8. admire

**Exercise 5:** 1. before 2. policeman 3. evidence 4. lover
5. Suddenly 6. turned 7. later

**Exercise 6:** 1. silence 2. seriousness 3. death 4. openness
5. illness 6. fun 7. anger 8. jealousy

**Exercise 7:** 1. arrive 2. all 3. uniform 4. front 5. some
6. anything 7. no

**Exercise 8:** 1. to 2. of 3. with 4. about 5. of 6. in 7. at

**Exercise 9:** 1. broke 2. was 3. entered 4. cut 5. that
6. think 7. anything

**Exercise 10:** 1. wrote 2. tried 3. ate 4. spoke 5. swore
6. went
**Lösung:** weapon

**Exercise 11:** 1. Someone opened the window from the inside.
2. Someone cut the telephone line outside.
3. There was only a power cut at the hotel.
4. Nathan is shocked to see his wife arrested.
5. A kitchen knife was the murder weapon.

**Exercise 12:** 1. d 2. a 3. b 4. f 5. c 6. e

**Exercise 13:** 1. Laureen's brother visits her in jail.
2. I had nothing to do with the burglary.
3. Laureen signed a contract.
4. He bought the hotel at a cheap price.
5. Edward knows nothing/doesn't know anything about the agreement.

# Final Test

**Exercise 1:** 1. picks up 2. dial tone 3. mobile phone 4. call 5. line 6. dials

**Exercise 2:** 1. I can't 2. I won't 3. I don't 4. you aren't 5. we couldn't 6. it isn't

**Exercise 3:** 1. They go there to celebrate their silver wedding anniversary.
2. Jack is a photographer.
3. He hears an American voice shouting Scarlet's name.
4. No, there was no sequel.
5. She looks at Jack's photographs on her computer.
6. He thinks Scarlet is staying at a hotel there.

**Exercise 4:** 1. true 2. false 3. false 4. false 5. true 6. true

**Exercise 5:** 1. Scarlet is tall and has blond, curly hair.
2. George does not often talk to strangers.
3. Juliet finds it easy to make friends.
4. The killer struck in the massage room.
5. The camera case is an important clue.
6. The Stubbs' son knows a lot about computers.

**Exercise 6:** 1. bet 2. brought 3. went 4. swore 5. kept 6. left 7. spoke 8. caught 9. struck 10. spread 11. worried 12. hit

**Exercise 7:** 1. b 2. b 3. a 4. a 5. b 6. a

**Exercise 8:** 1. f 2. c 3. e 4. b 5. g 6. a 7. d

**Exercise 9:** 1. into 2. up 3. to 4. across 5. of 6. for 7. in

**Exercise 10:** 1. details 2. policies 3. – 4. women 5. holidays
6. – 7. men 8. employees 9. addresses 10. –

# Glossary

⚡ = umgangssprachlich
*pl* = Plural

| | |
|---|---|
| abbey | Abtei |
| to accuse sb. | jmd. beschuldigen |
| acquaintance | Bekannte(r), Bekanntschaft |
| to admire | bewundern |
| to admit | zugeben |
| agreement | *hier*: Abmachung; Zustimmung |
| airy | luftig |
| ambulance | Krankenwagen |
| amount | Betrag, Menge |
| ankle | Knöchel |
| to announce | verkünden; ankündigen |
| annoying | ärgerlich, nervig |
| antiques dealer | Antiquitätenhändler(in) |
| appliance | Gerät |
| to approach | sich nähern |
| argument | *hier*: Streit, Auseinandersetzung |
| to arrest | verhaften |
| to assault | angreifen |
| associate | Geschäftspartner(in) |

| | |
|---|---|
| astonishment | Erstaunen |
| at once | sofort |
| attempt | Versuch |
| attempted murder | versuchter Mord |
| attendant | *hier*: Bademeister(in); Aufseher(in) |
| at the top of one's voice | aus vollem Hals, mit lauter Stimme |
| attic | Dachboden |
| to attract | anlocken, anziehen |
| back-up | *hier*: Unterstützung |
| bank statement | Kontoauszug |
| to be all ears | ganz Ohr sein |
| to be a mess | sehr unordentlich sein |
| to beat (beat, beaten) up | zusammenschlagen |
| bed sheet | Bettuch, Bettlaken |
| to be in touch | sich (wieder) melden |
| to be scared of heights | Höhenangst haben |
| besides | außerdem |
| to bet | wetten |
| to betray | verraten |
| to be used to sth. | (an) etw. gewöhnt sein |
| bill | Rechnung; Geldschein |
| blackberry | Brombeere |
| blessing | Segen |
| to blink | blinzeln |
| body wrap | Ganzkörperpackung |
| bolt of lightning | Blitz |
| to brake | bremsen |
| brave | mutig |
| break | *hier*: Durchbruch; Urlaub |
| to bring to mind | in Erinnerung rufen |
| bully | Rüpel |

| | |
|---|---|
| to bump into sb. | mit jmd. zusammenstoßen |
| burglar | Einbrecher(in) |
| burglary | Einbruch |
| to burgle a house | in ein Haus einbrechen |
| to cancel | absagen |
| candlestick | Kerzenständer |
| to carry on | fortfahren, weitermachen |
| carving | Schnitzerei |
| case | Fall; Tasche, Hülle |
| to cause | verursachen |
| to catch sb.'s eye | jmd. ins Auge fallen |
| celebrity gossip | Promiklatsch |
| challenge | Herausforderung |
| chandelier | Kronleuchter |
| to change one's mind | es sich anders überlegen |
| to change the subject | das Thema wechseln |
| channel | Kanal |
| to charge sb. (with sth.) | jmd. (wegen etw.) anzeigen, anklagen |
| cheerful(ly) | fröhlich, heiter |
| chemist | Apotheke |
| chimney | Schornstein |
| to chew | kauen |
| circumstantial evidence | Indizienbeweis |
| to claim | behaupten |
| cling film | Plastikfolie, Frischhaltefolie |
| clue | Hinweis, Spur |
| coal | Kohle |
| coated with | überzogen mit |
| coincidence | Zufall |

| | |
|---|---|
| to collapse | zusammenbrechen |
| collar | Kragen |
| community | Gemeinde |
| to complain | sich beschweren |
| complaint | Beschwerde |
| to confess | gestehen; beichten |
| to confirm | bestätigen |
| confirmation | Bestätigung |
| confused | verwirrt |
| consecutive | aufeinanderfolgend |
| to consider | überlegen |
| constable | Polizist(in) |
| convinced | überzeugt |
| convincing | überzeugend |
| counter | Theke, Ladentheke |
| court | Gericht, Hof |
| crime scene | Tatort |
| criminal record | Vorstrafenregister |
| crowd | Menschenmenge |
| crowded | gedrängt, überfüllt |
| cruel | grausam |
| ⚡ culture vulture | Kulturfanatiker(in) |
| curious | neugierig |
| current | aktuell |
| custard tart | Vanilletörtchen |
| cute | niedlich |
| ⚡ damned | verdammt |
| debt | Schulden |
| to dedicate | widmen |
| degree | *hier*: Hochschulabschluss; Grad |

| | |
|---|---|
| delight | Freude, Entzücken |
| delighted | erfreut, entzückt |
| to deny | leugnen |
| to deserve | verdienen |
| dial tone | Freizeichen |
| diary | Tagebuch |
| ⚡ to dig (dug, dug) into | sich stürzen auf |
| digoxin | Digoxin (aus Fingerhut gewonnener giftiger Wirkstoff) |
| dimple | Grübchen |
| direction | Richtung |
| disbelief | Fassungslosigkeit, Ungläubigkeit |
| to disturb | stören |
| to do sb. a favour | jmd. einen Gefallen tun |
| dozen | Dutzend |
| dressing gown | Bademantel |
| driveway | Einfahrt |
| to drop sb. off | jmd. absetzen |
| elderly | älter |
| embarrassed | verlegen |
| employee | Angestellte(r) |
| to enjoy sth. | etw. genießen, Freude an etw. haben |
| enormous | riesig, enorm |
| entrance | Eingang |
| envelope | Briefumschlag |
| evidence | Beweis(e) |
| to examine | untersuchen |
| to exclaim | (aus)rufen |
| execution | Hinrichtung |
| exhibition | Ausstellung |

| | |
|---|---|
| fake | gefälscht, falsch |
| file | Akte; Datei |
| filing cabinet | Aktenschrank |
| fist | Faust |
| to flash | aufleuchten, blinken |
| flat(ly) | flach, platt; ausdruckslos |
| floorboard | Diele(nbrett) |
| flower bed | Blumenbeet |
| forensics | Spurensicherung |
| forensic scientist | Gerichtsmediziner(in) |
| for the time being | einstweilen |
| foxglove | Fingerhut (Pflanze) |
| to frame sb. | jmd. etw. anhängen |
| from head to toe | von Kopf bis Fuß |
| to frown | die Stirn runzeln |
| funeral | Beerdigung |
| to gain | erlangen; profitieren |
| gap | Lücke |
| to gasp | keuchen, nach Luft schnappen |
| gay | homosexuell, schwul |
| gently | sanft, zärtlich |
| gift | Geschenk |
| gloves pl | Handschuhe |
| to grab | greifen, packen |
| to graduate | einen Hochschulabschluss erwerben |
| to groan | stöhnen, ächzen |
| grocery shop | Lebensmittelgeschäft |
| to grunt | brummeln; grunzen |
| ⚡ guys pl | Leute |
| half-day closing | halber freier Tag |

| | |
|---|---|
| halo | Heiligenschein |
| handcuffs *pl* | Handschellen |
| handle | Griff |
| ⚡ to have a lie-in | ausschlafen |
| to head for | zusteuern auf |
| headline | Schlagzeile |
| heart attack | Herzinfarkt |
| hoax | Streich, Zeitungsente |
| to howl | heulen |
| humiliating | demütigend, erniedrigend |
| I'm afraid … | Es tut mir leid, aber … |
| ice bucket | Eiskübel |
| icing | Zuckerguss |
| impatient(ly) | ungeduldig |
| to impress | beeindrucken |
| impressive | beeindruckend |
| to improve | besser werden |
| in advance | im Voraus |
| incredibly | unglaublich |
| infusion | *hier*: Aufguss |
| ingredient | Zutat |
| inheritance | Erbe |
| injured | verletzt |
| innocent(ly) | unschuldig |
| to insist | beharren, bestehen auf |
| insurance company | Versicherungsgesellschaft |
| insurance policy | Versicherungspolice |
| in the meantime | in der Zwischenzeit |
| to invent | erfinden |
| investigation | Ermittlung, Untersuchung |

| | |
|---|---|
| invisible | unsichtbar |
| involved | beteiligt |
| irritated | verärgert, genervt |
| item | Gegenstand, Artikel |
| jar | Einmachglas |
| jaw | Kiefer |
| jealous (of) | eifersüchtig (auf), neidisch (auf) |
| to jeer | johlen |
| to jump | *hier*: zusammenzucken; springen |
| kidney | Niere |
| kidney failure | Nierenversagen |
| to kill two birds with one stone | zwei Fliegen mit einer Klappe schlagen |
| to kneel (knelt, knelt) | knien, sich hinknien |
| lace curtain | Spitzengardine |
| land register | Grundbuch |
| last will and testament | Testament |
| late | *hier*: verstorben; spät |
| law | Gesetz |
| lawyer | Anwalt, Anwältin |
| leather-bound | in Leder gebunden |
| leaves *pl* | Blätter |
| legal aid | Rechtshilfe |
| lighter | Feuerzeug |
| lilac | Flieder |
| to line | säumen |
| to live on sth. | von etw. leben |
| locals *pl* | Einheimische |
| locker | Spind, Schließfach |
| locksmith | Schlosser |

| | |
|---|---|
| to lose (lost, lost) weight | abnehmen |
| to make a fool of sb. | jmd. zum Narren halten |
| magician | Zauberer |
| male | männlich |
| to manage sth. | etw. schaffen |
| marigold | Ringelblume |
| marriage | Ehe |
| master key | Hauptschlüssel |
| meanwhile | inzwischen, unterdessen |
| media stunt | PR-Gag |
| to meow | miauen |
| to mind sth. | etw. dagegen haben |
| to mist over | (sich) beschlagen |
| modest | bescheiden |
| mood | Laune |
| moustache | Schnurrbart |
| mug | Becher |
| to mumble | murmeln, brummen |
| to murder | (er)morden |
| murder mystery party | Krimispiel |
| ⚡ nap | Nickerchen |
| narrow | eng |
| nasty | scheußlich; gehässig |
| nausea | Übelkeit |
| newsflash | Kurzmeldung |
| to nod | nicken |
| no matter | egal |
| ⚡ nosy | neugierig |
| nowadays | heutzutage |
| to object | einwenden, protestieren |

| | |
|---|---|
| obvious(ly) | offensichtlich |
| occasional | gelegentlich |
| odd | seltsam, komisch |
| Oh dear! | Meine Güte!; Oje! |
| old-fashioned | altmodisch |
| ordinary | normal, gewöhnlich |
| oversight | Versehen |
| overtime | Überstunden |
| pale | blass, bleich |
| paramedic | Rettungssanitäter(in) |
| to pass | *hier*: geben, reichen; vorbeigehen |
| passion | Leidenschaft |
| to pat | tätscheln |
| to peek | spähen, gucken |
| peony | Pfingstrose |
| pew | Kirchenbank |
| pile | Stapel, Haufen |
| pillow | Kissen, Kopfkissen |
| plenty | viel, eine Menge |
| poison | Gift |
| to poison sb. | jmd. vergiften |
| posh | vornehm, schick |
| potassium | Kalium |
| to pour | einschenken, schütten |
| power cut | Stromausfall |
| Practice makes perfect. | Übung macht den Meister. |
| to pretend | vorgeben, vortäuschen |
| prime suspect | Hauptverdächtiger |
| property | *hier*: Eigenschaft; Eigentum |
| to prove | beweisen |

| | |
|---|---|
| purchase | Kauf |
| to question | befragen |
| questioning | Verhör, Befragung |
| rage | Wut(anfall), Zorn |
| to raise sth. | etw. (an)heben; erhöhen |
| to raise the alarm | Alarm schlagen |
| raspberry | Himbeere |
| rather | *hier*: lieber; ziemlich |
| to rattle | klappern, rütteln |
| receipt | Quittung |
| recent(ly) | kürzlich, jüngst |
| to recognize | (wieder)erkennen |
| record | Aufzeichnung, Aufnahme |
| to redecorate | renovieren |
| red herring | falsche Fährte |
| to reflect | zeigen, zum Ausdruck bringen |
| to reject sb. | jmd. zurückweisen |
| to release | freigeben, freilassen |
| relief | Erleichterung |
| to remind sb. | jmd. erinnern (an) |
| to report | melden, berichten; anzeigen |
| to research | untersuchen, erforschen |
| to resist | widerstehen |
| resolution | Bildauflösung |
| rest | *hier*: Ruhe, Pause |
| to rest | (sich) (aus)ruhen |
| to reveal | zum Vorschein bringen, zeigen |
| revenge | Rache |
| reverend | Pfarrer(in), Pastor(in) |
| Roman Bath | Römisches Bad |

| | |
|---|---|
| root | Wurzel |
| rude | grob, unhöflich |
| rug | kleiner Teppich, Vorleger |
| rumble of thunder | Donnergrollen |
| to rush | eilen, rasen |
| salary | Lohn |
| salmon | Lachs |
| scone | brötchenartiges Teegebäck |
| to scratch | kratzen |
| ⚡ secretive | geheimnistuerisch |
| to sedure | verführen |
| semi-detached (house) | Doppelhaushälfte |
| sensation | *hier:* Empfindung, Gefühl |
| sentence | *hier:* Strafe; Satz |
| sergeant | Polizeimeister(in) |
| serious | ernst |
| shift | Schicht |
| shiny | glänzend, leuchtend |
| to shiver | erschauern, zittern |
| to shrug (one's shoulders) | die Achseln zucken |
| sight | Sehenswürdigkeit; Anblick |
| sincere | aufrichtig |
| sink | Spülbecken |
| to sip | nippen, trinken |
| to slam the door | die Tür zuknallen |
| sleeping partner | stille(r) Teilhaber(in) |
| slim | schlank |
| smart | *hier:* schick; schlau |
| smoking gun | *hier:* eindeutiger Beweis |
| to snap | *hier:* anschnauzen, blaffen |

| | |
|---|---|
| to solve | lösen; aufklären |
| soul | Seele |
| soundly | *hier*: fest; gründlich |
| to spot sth. | etw. entdecken |
| to spread | sich verbreiten |
| to stab | (er)stechen, einstechen auf |
| stab wound | Stichwunde |
| staff | Mitarbeiter(team) |
| stained-glass window | Buntglasfenster |
| staircase | Treppe |
| to stare | starren |
| state | Zustand |
| to state | angeben, feststellen |
| stately home | Herrenhaus |
| statement | Aussage, Erklärung |
| stern(ly) | streng |
| stomach | Bauch, Magen |
| to strangle | erwürgen |
| to stretch | (sich) strecken |
| stretcher | Tragbahre |
| to strike | (zu)schlagen |
| to stroke | streicheln |
| struggle | Kampf, Streit |
| to struggle | kämpfen |
| superficial | oberflächlich |
| superior | Vorgesetzte(r) |
| to suppose | annehmen, vermuten |
| surrounded by | umgeben von |
| surveillance | Überwachung |
| suspect | Verdächtige(r) |
| to suspect | verdächtigen, einen Verdacht haben |

| | |
|---|---|
| suspicious(ly) | verdächtig; misstrauisch |
| to swear (swore, sworn) | schwören; fluchen |
| sympathetically | mitfühlend, verständnisvoll |
| tape | (Video-)Band, Kassette |
| taxes *pl* | Steuern |
| ⚡ taxman | Finanzamt |
| that very day | eben an jenem Tag |
| That's your loss! | Das ist deine Sache! |
| The penny drops. | Der Groschen fällt. |
| theft | Diebstahl |
| thermal spa | Thermalbad |
| they say | *hier*: es heißt, alle sagen |
| thief, thieves *pl* | Dieb(in) |
| throat | Hals |
| to throw (threw, thrown) | werfen |
| tin | Dose, Büchse |
| tip | *hier*: Trinkgeld |
| tissue | Papiertaschentuch |
| to toast to sth. | auf etw. anstoßen |
| torn | zerrissen |
| to transfer | *hier*: überweisen; übertragen |
| trap | Falle |
| to treat | behandeln |
| to treat oneself to sth. | sich etw. gönnen |
| to trust | (ver)trauen |
| trustworthy | vertrauenswürdig |
| to turn red | rot werden, erröten |
| twin beds *pl* | zwei Einzelbetten |
| twisted | verdreht, verstaucht |
| unemployed | arbeitslos |
| upset | aufgeregt, verärgert |

| | |
|---|---|
| used to do sth. | etw. (früher) getan haben |
| valuable | wertvoll |
| vicarage | Pfarrhaus |
| victim | Opfer |
| villain | Bösewicht, Schurke |
| violence | Gewalt |
| to wave | schwenken; winken |
| wedding anniversary | Hochzeitstag |
| what's more | außerdem, vor allem |
| to whisper | flüstern |
| wig | Perücke |
| to wink | zwinkern |
| to wipe | (ab)wischen |
| witness | Zeuge/Zeugin |
| wrist | Handgelenk |
| to yawn | gähnen |

 # List of Exercises

|   | Focus | Exercise | Page |
|---|-------|----------|------|
| **Murder at Teatime** | | | |
| 1 | Grammar | Simple Past | 11 |
| 2 | Grammar | Questions | 14 |
| 3 | Vocabulary | Translation | 17 |
| 4 | Grammar | Negation | 20 |
| 5 | Grammar | Choose the correct alternative | 22 |
| 6 | Grammar | Prepositions | 26 |
| 7 | Grammar | Adjectives | 28 |
| 8 | Grammar | Present Continuous | 31 |
| 9 | Vocabulary | Fill in the blanks | 33 |
| 10 | Comprehension | Unscramble the sentences | 37 |
| **A Model Murder** | | | |
| 1 | Grammar | Adjectives | 45 |
| 2 | Comprehension | True or false? | 47 |
| 3 | Grammar | Verb forms | 50 |
| 4 | Grammar | Prepositions | 53 |
| 5 | Vocabulary | Translation | 57 |
| 6 | Vocabulary | Choose the correct alternative | 59 |
| 7 | Vocabulary | Odd one out | 61 |
| 8 | Comprehension | Fill in the blanks | 63 |
| 9 | Grammar | Choose the correct alternative | 66 |

|   | Focus | Exercise | Page |
|---|-------|----------|------|
| 10 | Vocabulary | Unscramble the sentences | 70 |
| 11 | Comprehension | Questions about the text | 76 |
| 12 | Vocabulary | Definitions | 80 |
| 13 | Grammar | Verb forms | 82 |

## A Family Affair

|   | Focus | Exercise | Page |
|---|-------|----------|------|
| 1 | Comprehension | True or false? | 89 |
| 2 | Grammar | Verb forms | 91 |
| 3 | Grammar | Negation | 93 |
| 4 | Grammar | Verb forms | 96 |
| 5 | Vocabulary | Fill in the blanks | 98 |
| 6 | Grammar | Adjectives and nouns | 101 |
| 7 | Vocabulary | Choose the correct alternative | 102 |
| 8 | Grammar | Prepositions | 106 |
| 9 | Grammar | Choose the correct alternative | 110 |
| 10 | Grammar | Simple Past | 113 |
| 11 | Vocabulary | Unscramble the sentences | 115 |
| 12 | Vocabulary | In other words | 118 |
| 13 | Vocabulary | Translation | 121 |

## Final Test

|   | Focus | Exercise | Page |
|---|-------|----------|------|
| 1 | Vocabulary | Unscramble the words | 128 |
| 2 | Grammar | Short answers | 128 |
| 3 | Comprehension | Reading comprehension | 129 |
| 4 | Comprehension | True or false? | 129 |
| 5 | Vocabulary | Translation | 130 |
| 6 | Grammar | Simple Past | 130 |
| 7 | Grammar | Choose the correct alternative | 131 |
| 8 | Vocabulary | Phrasal Verbs | 131 |
| 9 | Grammar | Prepositions | 132 |
| 10 | Grammar | Plural | 132 |

# Notizen